Pancakes

Pancakes

from FLAPJACKS to CRÊPES

by

Dorian Leigh Parker

Illustrations by Sally Sturman

Clarkson N. Potter, Inc./Publishers
DISTRIBUTED BY CROWN PUBLISHERS, INC.
NEW YORK

This book could not have existed without the gallant efforts of my editor,
Pam Krauss, and the echelons behind her.

I owe thanks to Bert Greene and his publisher, Workman;
to Judith Olney and her publisher, Atheneum; to Barbara Farr and Keats Publishing;
to Jack Lirio and his publisher, William Morrow, for the permission
to print recipes from their books.

~

Grateful acknowledgment is given for permission to reprint the following:

Judith Olney, "Filigreed Crêpes" from *Summer Food.* Copyright © 1979 Judith Olney.
Reprinted with the permission of Atheneum Publishers, Inc.

Barbara Farr, "Super Pancake Mix" from *Super Soy!* Copyright © 1976 Barbara Farr.
All rights reserved. Reprinted with the permission of Keats Publishing, Inc.

Jack Lirio, "A Fat Broiled Pancake with Pecans" from *Cooking with Jack Lirio.*
Copyright © 1982 by Jack Lirio. Reprinted with the permission of William Morrow & Co.

Bert Greene, "A Spinach Pancake" from *Greene on Greens.* Copyright © 1984
Bert Greene. Reprinted with the permission of Bert Greene.

Published by Clarkson N. Potter, Inc., 225 Park Avenue South, New York, New York
10003, and represented in Canada by the Canadian MANDA Group.
CLARKSON N. POTTER, POTTER, and colophon are trademarks of
Clarkson N. Potter, Inc.

Manufactured in the United States of America

Design by Gael Towey and Barbara Peck

Library of Congress Cataloging-in-Publication Data
Parker, Dorian Leigh, 1920–
Pancakes : from flapjacks to crêpes.
Includes index.
1. Pancakes, waffles, etc. I. Title.
TX770.P34P37 1987   641.8   86–25569
ISBN 0-517-56136-0
10 9 8 7 6 5 4 3 2 1
First Edition

~

To my sisters,
Florian, Georgibell, and Suzy,
in memory of those Texan women,
our valiant forebears

Contents

~

Introduction 1

~

Breakfast Pancakes 11

~

Savory Pancakes 43

~

Dessert Pancakes 78

~

Index 120

Introduction

When I was a child, the best days began with a crash from the kitchen. It was my father, knocking over all the pans in the kitchen closet to unearth the heavy, cast-iron pancake griddle, always at the bottom of the pile of black skillets. Next (to get us definitely out of bed) came the smell of bacon and sausages—tiny, finger-length ones, cooked first to season the griddle. ～ The batter had been made the night before—always with buttermilk and always put to refrigerate overnight in a narrow-necked milk bottle. Nowadays, a 1-liter Italian wine carafe serves the same purpose, since glass milk bottles have vanished along with that buttermilk—flecked with butter from the churning. ～ The grease from the meat was drained into an empty can, four dollops of batter were poured on the hot griddle and, when bubbles began to form, were turned with a flexible spatula (familiarly called "the pancake turner"). By the time a stack of twelve pancakes had accumulated, four of us were at the table, my mother having always preferred bed to breakfast. ～ On the table next to the little log cabin of maple syrup was a comb of honey, dark and tasting of orange blossoms. After the feast, by chewing furiously, I could keep a wad of beeswax in my mouth for quite a while before it turned dry and crumbly. ~ This small pleasure seems to have diminished with age, in contrast to that of eating pancakes. This festive, comforting food always makes me feel warm and nostalgic. Judging by the fact that there was always a crowd before the windows of Child's restaurants, where for years a white-coated man in chef's hat kept golden butter cakes flipping on a vast griddle, I share this emotion with most people. Prehistorians differ drastically as to the date of man's beginning attempts at cooking, but most put the use of fire at about 500,000 years ago, a date that varies with the geographic regions. Surely the hottest climates discovered the sun as a source of energy before they controlled fire. ~ Water and a fistful of pounded grain poured upon a hot rock in the sun must have been the world's first pancake, the very first bread. To this day in North Africa a kind of pancake bread is baked upon the desert sand, and the unleavened pancake is still eaten in many parts of the world: the Mexican tortilla, the chapati and paratha of India, the scallion and Mandarin pancakes of China, and the warka of Morocco. In their simplest form or the most elaborate, pancakes figure in every cuisine. They are a favorite food with rich and poor alike,

knowing no such snobbish division as that between the overre-
fined white bread of upper society and the dark, chewy loaf of the
peasant, which used to exist in Western civilization. ⌁ In
Egypt, in the excavated tombs, stones for grinding grain have
been found, and pictorial proof on the walls, dated from 8000 B.C.,
shows that pancakes were important in the ancient Egyptian diet.
Recorded feasts from the time of Plato featured pancakes. More
than three centuries later, a pancake recipe appeared in a collection of manuscripts given the title *De Re Coquinaria,* attributed
to Apicius, a notorious epicure. His recipe for pancakes, trans-
lated many times since, is identical to the basic one of today—
eggs, flour, and milk—and is distinguished only by his suggestion
that they be served with a syrup of honey mixed with pepper.
The story goes that Apicius, a lavish giver of banquets, reached
a time when he calculated that he did not have enough gold to
continue eating in the style to which he had accustomed his
friends, and so committed suicide. ⌁ Ancient cultures observed
seedtime and harvest with religious ceremonies involving pancakes; the early Slavonic tribes held these round cakes to be a
symbol of their sun god. After the founding of Christianity these

feasts were celebrated in the church calendar as religious rites and after the Reformation as civil holidays. ⌇ The observance of Lent, a period of fasting and repentance before Easter, accumulated curious customs. Meat was not the only food to be forsworn, but also all of its by-products: eggs, milk, animal fats. Having no refrigeration, everyone made haste to eat up the perishables before Ash Wednesday, and what could be more logical than to eat, drink, and combine eggs, milk, and butter with a little flour and make merry pancakes? ⌇ In France, the second of February is Chandeleurs, Pancake Day. Many customs have grown up around this Lenten holiday, varying from province to province. In some, tossing a crêpe into the air with one hand and recatching it in the pan while holding a piece of money in the other hand assures the flipper a year without financial worries. Other localities conceal yards of fine thread in one of the crêpes, and the unsuspecting diner who consumes it is consoled with a prize—after he has bitten, of course. ⌇ In the Netherlands, pancakes are not just a Lenten tradition but also a pastime. Townships vie with one another in fanciful creations; some are gigantic, oven-baked, and puffy as soufflés, even decorated with icing. ⌇ In

England, on Shrove Tuesday before Lent there are pancake races and pancake-eating contests. In these last, the English are easily outdone by the Finns, who devour whole meals of *pannukakku* and pride themselves on outeating their neighbors. The quantity of pancakes consumed is also a matter of contest in Russia during Maslyenitsa, or Butter Week. As in France, everyone tries his hand at making blini, the Russian crêpe. ～ Pancake making has understandably become a fine craft, and the right equipment is very important. The pancake griddle comes in several shapes and varied materials. The rectangular type that fits over two burners is ideal, but the round griddle, while making fewer pancakes at a time, is just as efficient. I prefer black cast-iron griddles over the cast-aluminum ones, although they are a little more difficult to care for. Soapstone ones are the most desirable because they distribute the heat so evenly, but they are also the most expensive. Most electrical-appliance manufacturers make tabletop griddles that are simple to use but in my opinion are a bore to clean. A cast-iron skillet of 9- to 10-inch diameter may be substituted for the griddle, and I have often used my cherished paella pan, which works very well. ～ Crêpes, however, must be made in a crêpe pan or small frying pan, heavy enough to distribute heat evenly but light enough to maneuver easily. The more desirable, classic crêpe pan can be found at any good cooking equipment or kitchen supply shop. Most are of black iron, but pans with special nonstick finishes are available and, although more expensive, do not need the care that cast iron requires. ⁓ Crêpe pans vary from 5 to 8 inches across, and the inside diameter of the pan determines the exact size of the finished crêpe. My favorite one is 5½ inches in diameter, which is a convenient size for both entrée and dessert dishes. ⁓ To season a griddle, crêpe pan, or skillet of black iron, impregnate a paper towel with vegetable oil and wipe the cooking surface. (I avoid olive oil for this because it leaves a flavor.) Pour in more oil, ⅛-inch deep, and set the pan over medium heat for 15 minutes. Let it cool, pour out any excess oil, and wipe it clean with paper towels. ⁓ The griddle or frying pan should also be greased lightly each time it is used. I prefer to use vegetable oil, brushed on with a pastry brush, for this purpose, although in some instances I have indicated that butter or bacon fat will give a more authentic flavor to the pancakes. Virtually any type of oil or shortening is acceptable, and should be reapplied to the surface of the griddle frequently, to prevent sticking. If, despite your preparations, the batter has stuck in places and left crusts, scour the pan with coarse salt—not a metal abrasive or powder. If absolutely necessary, wash it in hot soapy water, being sure to dry thoroughly, and season again. ~ For cooks who are not fortunate enough to own an electric mixer, for combining pancake ingredients an electric hand beater or wire whisk is just as good, if slower. Food processors can also be used for many recipes. In a few instances I have noted that ingredients are to be combined "by hand," and this instruction should be heeded, as it is essential to the batter's consistency. ~ For the Swedish pancakes on page 94, a special pan, called *plättpan*, is required. It is round and fits over any burner, and usually is made of cast iron; it needs the same care as black iron skillets, griddles, or crêpe pans. Kitchen specialty shops also have these pans in the nonstick finishes. Their seven small round indentations are perfect with any pancake batter to make uniformly shaped cakes that are a good size for hors d'oeuvres. ~ All measurements in these recipes are level. I prefer the European system of weighing ingredients as being more accurate, but a set of nested, stainless steel measuring cups is excellent. Try to find them with a reasonable handle, instead of the little lip that allows the batter to run over your fingers. For 2-tablespoon amounts, the plastic measure that comes with ground coffee is just right, but half-filling a ¼-cup measure works fairly well. ⌒ To keep cooked pancakes warm as you cook the remaining batter, it is best to preheat the oven to warm, or 200° F., and place the cakes in an ovenproof dish or on a baking sheet, as each recipe directs. ⌒ Almost every cookbook, whether ethnic or general, contains recipes for pancakes and I have given only a sampling of the infinite variations. Fillings are often interchangeable and so are the occasions on which they are served. Nearly any sweet or savory sauce or filling can be combined with a pancake or crêpe to create new dishes.

Breakfast
PANCAKES

Breakfast in bed for schoolchildren? ~ To the outrage of my friends, my school-age children always had breakfast in bed because I had discovered that awakening them with a tray accomplished two things quickly: it assured me that they were awake and that they had time to eat. Pancakes, on the other hand, were eaten at the table and only when we had time to sit down and enjoy; consequently they became associated in our minds with unhurried pleasure and celebration. ~ In northern climates, a comforting and substantial breakfast is the rule and the grains most convenient to hand are stirred into the morning pancakes. Modern research has affirmed this tradition, telling us that a complex carbohydrate breakfast is more healthful than the bacon-and-eggs habit. In all but the crêpes recipes, up to one third of the unbleached, all-purpose flour can be replaced by other grains, and I sprinkle in every batter (even for my Queen of Sheba chocolate cake) 1 tablespoon of toasted wheat germ. You should experiment in your own kitchen with different combinations. ~ The storage of whole-grain flour is important; it should be kept dry and cool, and not in plastic bags. The best method I have found to keep flour of this sort from going rancid or attracting weevils is storing it in the refrigerator or freezer. ∼ Homemade syrups are quite easily prepared and taste far superior to commercial "maple" syrups. Syrups can be kept in glass jars in the refrigerator for 10 days without trouble, but the sugar may crystallize. If this occurs, bring the syrup to a boil in a heavy saucepan until the sugar dissolves. Honey that has thickened or turned to sugar may be heated in the jar in an inch or so of water in a small saucepan, just until it liquefies again. ∼ To can the Blueberry Syrup on page 31, or any other, for indefinite storage, pour it while hot into clean, hot, pint-size canning jars, leaving ½ inch of head space. Wipe the rims and put on two-piece lids. Set the jars on a rack in a deep kettle containing enough water at 190° F. to reach halfway up their sides. Add hot water (not hotter than 190° F.) to cover the jars by 2 inches. Set over heat, thermometer in place, and process at 190° F. for 30 minutes. Don't let the water boil. Cool the jars before storing.

Buttermilk Pancakes

S o necessary were my father's buttermilk pancakes to my happiness and well-being that this recipe was written into the diary I took with me when I went off to college. I was sure that the occasion would arise when I would be able to nourish my morale as well as my mind. Fortunately, I had free run of the dormitory kitchen on Sunday afternoons. ~ This is enough for four big appetites.

    2 cups unbleached, all-purpose flour
    1 teaspoon baking soda
    1 teaspoon baking powder
    1 tablespoon sugar
    1 large egg
    2 cups buttermilk, plus 2 additional tablespoons if necessary
    2 tablespoons unsalted butter, melted, or vegetable oil or
      bacon fat

Combine the flour, baking soda, baking powder, and sugar in a large bowl.

Break the egg into a 4-cup measure, add the buttermilk, and mix thoroughly. Add to the flour mixture and beat with a whisk or mixer until smooth. Pour into a covered container; refrigerate overnight.

Next morning, beat the batter thoroughly, adding up to 2 tablespoons of buttermilk as needed until the batter is of a pouring consistency. Stir in the melted butter, oil, or bacon fat.

Grease a griddle or skillet and heat over medium heat until a drop of water skates over the surface. Using a ¼-cup measure, pour the batter onto the hot griddle, leaving an inch between cakes for spreading. (If you like larger pancakes, use a larger measure or ladle for pouring.) Cook until bubbles appear, then turn with a spatula or pancake turner to brown the other side. Serve immediately, or keep warm in an ovenproof dish in a preheated 200° F. oven. Serve with honey or syrup.

Banana Buttermilk
Griddle Cakes

T*his is a confection rather than a pancake, a Cinderella-at-the-ball version of my father's buttermilk pancake. It is perfect for a lazy holiday breakfast or a Sunday-night supper. ~ This recipe serves four.*

 4   large eggs, separated
 3   tablespoons sugar
1½   cups buttermilk
 2   tablespoons unsalted butter, melted and cooled
 1   teaspoon vanilla or lemon extract
 2   teaspoons grated lemon rind
 2   cups coarsely chopped banana (about 3 medium bananas)
1½   cups cake flour
 1   teaspoon baking powder
 ½   teaspoon baking soda
 ¾   teaspoon cinnamon

In a large bowl, or food processor, beat the egg yolks with the sugar until pale yellow. Add the buttermilk, cooled butter, extract, rind, and banana. Combine thoroughly.

Sift the flour with the baking powder, soda, and cinnamon; mix into the banana mixture. In another bowl, whisk the egg whites until stiff but not dry, and fold into the batter.

Heat a griddle or skillet until a drop of water skates over the surface. Brush lightly with oil or butter. Using a ¼-cup measure, pour the batter onto the griddle and cook until brown. Turn and brown the other side. Keep the cooked griddle cakes warm on an ovenproof plate in a 200° F. oven, buttering each cake as done. Serve with fruit preserves or honey.

Vermont Flannel Cakes

his is an interesting variation on the Pennsylvania Dutch flannel cakes. I suppose, like the names "flapjacks" and "johnnycakes," the origin of "flannel cakes" as a name for griddle cakes is lost in history. ~ This will serve four.

    1 cup quick oats (*not* instant)
    2 cups buttermilk
    1 tablespoon sugar
    1 teaspoon baking soda
   ¾ cup unbleached, all-purpose flour
    2 small eggs
       Cranberry Applesauce

In a large bowl, soak the oatmeal in the buttermilk for 15 minutes. It will thicken slightly.

Sift the sugar, soda, and flour together and stir into the oat mixture. Beat in the eggs, mixing thoroughly, and let the batter rest 15 minutes. It should be like heavy cream in consistency. If it is too thin, add a sprinkle of flour; if too thick, thin with a little buttermilk.

Heat a griddle or skillet over medium heat until a drop of water skates over the surface. Brush with vegetable oil and reduce the heat to low. Using a ½-cup measure, pour out rounds and brown on both sides. Butter the cakes as made and keep them warm in an ovenproof dish in a 200° F. oven. Serve with Cranberry Applesauce.

CRANBERRY APPLESAUCE
~

- 1 pound Golden Delicious apples
  (about 3 large apples)
- 4 tablespoons sugar
- 2 cups water
- 1 (12-ounce) package cranberries

Peel and core the apples. Slice thinly and combine with the sugar and water in a heavy saucepan. Bring to a boil, reduce the heat, cover, and cook, adding more hot water if necessary to keep the apples from sticking. When they are very soft, in about 12 minutes, pour in the cranberries and stir to distribute evenly. Cover again and cook about 6 minutes, until the cranberries begin to burst. Uncover and continue to cook over a low flame until all the cranberries have opened, adding more hot water as needed. Serve hot. ~ This recipe makes about 3 cups.

Super Blueberry Pancakes

T his is the most health-conscious recipe I have ever known. With its five different flours, enriched by wheat germ and lecithin, it is guaranteed to put your athletes, whether the indoor or outdoor type, into champion shape. The best news is that the pancake mix can be kept in an airtight container in the freezer for upward of two months, needing only a few minutes of preparation before the batter is ready to pour on the griddle. Most large health food stores will carry all these ingredients. ∼ This recipe makes four servings.

> 1 cup Super Pancake Mix
>   Sea salt to taste (optional)
> 1 teaspoon baking powder
> 3 eggs
> ¾ cup skim milk
> 1 cup blueberries
>   Yogurt (optional)
> ¼ cup additional blueberries for garnish (optional)

Beat together all the ingredients (except the yogurt and blueberries) in a food processor or mixer, or whisk by hand in a large bowl. Stir in the blueberries. Let the batter stand 1 hour.

Over moderate heat, warm the griddle or skillet until a drop of water skids over the surface.

Using a half-filled ¼-cup measure for each pancake, pour the batter on the griddle, turning to brown the second side when bubbles appear on the surface. Keep the pancakes warm in a 200° F. oven until ready to serve. Serve with yogurt if desired, sprinkled with a few extra blueberries.

SUPER PANCAKE MIX

~

3 cups whole-wheat flour

1 cup soy flour

1 cup buckwheat flour

1 cup wheat germ

½ cup cornmeal (preferably yellow)

½ cup brown rice flour

½ cup brewer's yeast

½ cup powdered lecithin

In a large mixing bowl, combine all the ingredients thoroughly. Place in an airtight container and store in the refrigerator for no longer than 10 days, or in the freezer for up to 2 months. ~ This recipe makes 8 cups, enough for 8 batches of Super Pancakes.

Pumpkin Pancakes

Because of her grandchildren's insatiable appetite for bread and butter and cinnamon sugar, my grandmother kept a Mason jar of sugar mixed with cinnamon and a vanilla bean next to her jar of sugar. As an added refinement, she kept sticks of whole cinnamon in the cinnamon sugar jar. This magic mix was used in her fruitcakes and gingerbread sticks, both specialités de la maison. ⌒ Bacon grease was the fat used for cooking, since the supply was constant and cheap. Cholesterol watchers should substitute vegetable oil. ⌒ This is enough for two or three people; the recipe may be doubled or tripled.

   1 cup pumpkin purée
      Molasses to taste (optional)
   ½ cup unbleached, all-purpose flour
   ½ teaspoon ground allspice
   ½ teaspoon baking powder
   1 large egg, beaten
      Bacon grease or oil, for griddle
      Softened butter
      Cinnamon Syrup

Place the pumpkin purée in a large bowl and sweeten to taste with molasses if desired. Sift the flour, allspice, and baking powder together and stir into the purée, mixing well. Beat in the egg and let stand at least 30 minutes.

Heat the griddle over medium heat until a drop of water skates over the surface. Grease lightly. Drop the batter by tablespoonfuls and brown the cakes on both sides. Serve immediately with the softened butter and cinnamon syrup.

CINNAMON SYRUP

~

¾ cup sugar

1 teaspoon ground cinnamon

½ cup water

    3-inch piece of cinnamon stick

Mix the sugar with the cinnamon and combine with the measured water in a small heavy saucepan. Bring to a boil, then lower the heat. Add the cinnamon stick and continue cooking until a candy thermometer registers 220° F, about 5 to 8 minutes. Serve warm. ~ This recipe makes about ½ cup.

Welsh Currant Cakes

*A*lthough Wales is far from Yorkshire, these Welsh pancakes, called cacen-gri, are the sort of hearty breakfast I can imagine the farmers in James Herriot's beloved books eating before they go out into a snowstorm to rescue their sheep. ⌐ This should serve four to six people.

3½ cups unbleached, all-purpose flour
1 teaspoon baking powder
½ teaspoon mace
6 tablespoons butter
3 tablespoons milk plus 1 tablespoon more, if needed
1 large egg
3 tablespoons sugar
¼ cup dried currants

In a large bowl, sift the flour with the baking powder and mace. Rub in the butter with your fingers. Beat the milk with the egg and stir into the flour mixture. Add the sugar and currants, and combine.

Turn the dough out onto a lightly floured surface and knead for 2 minutes. If the dough is too stiff to handle easily, knead in a little more milk, drop by drop. Divide the dough into 12 equal parts.

Roll each segment of dough into a round 8 inches in diameter, covering remaining dough with a cloth. Over a moderate heat, heat the griddle or skillet until a drop of water races over the surface. Brown each cake on both sides and butter immediately. Make stacks of 6 on an ovenproof dish and keep in a 200° F. oven until all are ready.

To serve, cut each stack in wedges and sprinkle with more sugar before serving.

Cottage Cheese Pancakes

I *first ate these delicious pancakes in a dairy restaurant in downtown New York City. The three others at the table ate blintzes while I waited the forewarned twenty minutes for my order. Alas, when it came everyone had finished theirs and I had to give tastes to them all, leaving me with one lonely cake. ~ This recipe should not be doubled, but made afresh for every two servings.*

¾ cup large-curd cottage cheese
3 large eggs, separated
4 tablespoons unbleached, all-purpose flour
4 tablespoons sour cream
Fresh raspberries (optional)

Drain the cottage cheese in a sieve for a few minutes until it is dry of all liquid.

In a small bowl, whisk the egg yolks until lemon colored. In a larger bowl, combine the flour and cottage cheese, mixing thoroughly. Add the yolks and mix again. Beat the egg whites until stiff but not dry, and fold them gently into the cheese mixture.

Heat a griddle or skillet until a drop of water skates over the surface. Grease lightly with oil. Drop the batter by scant tablespoonfuls and brown on both sides. Place the finished cakes on paper towels while cooking the rest of the batter.

In the middle of each plate, place a heaping tablespoonful of sour cream and arrange the pancakes around it. Garnish with raspberries, if desired.

Bread Crumb Griddle Cakes

W hen it became known among my friends that I was writ-
ing a book on pancakes, there were only two reactions:
either, "What is there to say about pancakes?" or, "My
old———[fill in with aunt, mother, grandmother, neighbor] made
these wonderful original pancakes without much flour." I received three
different versions of the bread crumb pancake and combined them all
into this recipe. ～ This will feed four.

    1 cup soft bread crumbs, preferably whole wheat or
      pumpernickel
    1 cup buttermilk
    2 large eggs
    ½ teaspoon baking soda
    2 tablespoons brown sugar (light or dark)
    8 tablespoons unbleached, all-purpose flour, plus
      2 tablespoons extra, if needed
    1 cup puréed fruit (pages 110–112)

Soak the bread crumbs in the buttermilk for 2 to 3 hours or until
all the liquid is absorbed.

Beat the eggs with the soda and sugar and stir into the bread
crumb mixture. Add the flour slowly, one third at a time, beating
after each addition. The batter should be thick, about the
consistency of sour cream. If necessary, add a small amount of the
extra flour until this thickness is obtained.

Heat a griddle or skillet until a drop of water skates on the
surface. Drop the batter by heaping tablespoonfuls, flattening each
round to ⅛-inch thickness with the back of the spoon. Brown the
cakes on both sides and keep them warm in an ovenproof dish in a
200° F. oven until all are made. Top with fruit purée.

Frontier Flapjacks

s the name suggests, this might be the breakfast eaten by the family in the Little House on the Prairie, *or even by my grandmother in her youth. She was very proud to be a member of the Old Traildriver's Association in San Antonio. (It must have been a very small group since I have never heard of anyone else who belonged.) ⁓ This will serve six easily, and more if accompanied by eggs or sausages.*

1½ cups white or yellow cornmeal

2 tablespoons molasses or dark corn syrup

2 cups boiling water

5 large eggs

2 cups buttermilk

3 cups unbleached, all-purpose flour

2 tablespoons baking powder

½ teaspoon baking soda

⅓ cup butter, melted (or melted margarine or lard)

Place the cornmeal in a large mixing bowl. Stir the molasses or corn syrup into the boiling water, and pour over the cornmeal, stirring continuously and pressing out any lumps. Allow the batter to cool, then beat in the eggs, one at a time; add the buttermilk and beat until smooth.

Sift the flour, baking powder, and soda together and fold into the cornmeal mixture. Add the melted butter, blending carefully. Let stand for 1 hour.

Over moderate heat, heat a griddle or skillet until a drop of water skids over the surface. Grease lightly. Use ½ cup of batter for each cake, smoothing to a thickness of ⅛ inch with a small spatula. Brown on both sides and serve immediately with butter and brown sugar or with a light syrup.

Whole-Grain Griddle Cakes

T*his recipe is an example of how different grains of varying textures can be combined into a healthful flour. If you do not have a health food store conveniently near, the oat flour can be made by whirling oatmeal (of the rolled variety, not instant,) in your blender or food processor until it is homogeneous. I have used this method to make flour from bran flakes and even from shredded wheat biscuits, which I sometimes substitute equally for ½ cup of all-purpose flour in any of the breakfast pancake recipes, just to avoid monotony. When I don't have time to make Cranberry Syrup, these are also good with a dollop of sour cream sprinkled with cinnamon. ⁓ Serves four.*

> 1⅓ cups whole-wheat flour
> ⅔ cup unbleached, all-purpose flour
> ⅔ cup stone-ground cornmeal
> ⅔ cup oat flour (see headnote above)
> 1 tablespoon baking powder
> 2 teaspoons baking soda
> Pinch of salt (optional)
> ¾ cup unsalted butter or margarine
> 4 cups buttermilk
> 4 large eggs, lightly beaten
> ⅓ cup light molasses or corn syrup
> 1 cup butter, softened at room temperature
> Cranberry Syrup

Combine the dry ingredients in a large bowl and rub in the butter or margarine with your fingers. In another bowl, thoroughly mix together the buttermilk, eggs, and molasses or syrup; add to the dry mixture, stirring just until combined. Let it stand for 15 minutes, thinning with more buttermilk, if necessary, to a proper pouring consistency.

Heat a griddle or heavy skillet over medium heat, until a drop of water skates over the surface. Using a ½-cup measure, pour on the batter in 6-inch rounds. When the tops of the cakes are full of little holes, turn and brown the other sides. Slide onto an ovenproof platter and butter at once. Make stacks of 6 cakes and keep them warm in a 200° F. oven.

When ready to serve, cut each stack in 4 portions or wedges, and serve with Cranberry Syrup.

CRANBERRY SYRUP

2 cups sugar

⅔ cup water

1 (12-ounce) package cranberries

½ teaspoon ginger, nutmeg, or cinnamon (optional)

In a heavy saucepan, stir together the sugar and water. Bring them to a boil over medium heat and simmer over lowered heat for 10 minutes. Add the cranberries all at once and continue to cook over low heat until the berries have burst open. Remove from the heat and let cool 5 minutes. Stir in a teaspoon of your favorite spice, if desired. Serve at room temperature. ～ This recipe makes about 2 cups.

Skillet Cakes with Ham

When I think of Copenhagen, I have a memory of light reflecting from many surfaces: dazzling white of tiles, golden gleam of polished brass and copper, the satin glow of light lacquered wood, and the sparkling cleanliness everywhere. ⁓ The Danish people are noted for many foods—their pastry, their beer, their pork, and their not-to-be-forgotten pancakes. When two or three of these are combined, the result is wonderful. ⁓ This recipe is a Copenhagen specialty for four people.

    1 cup unbleached, all-purpose flour
    1 teaspoon sugar
    3 large eggs
    2 cups milk
    2 tablespoons butter
    ½ pound boiled or canned Danish ham, diced
    4 tablespoons vegetable oil
      Apple Cider Syrup

In a large bowl, whisk the flour and sugar into the eggs. Add the milk in a steady stream, beating continuously. Cover the bowl with a cloth and let it rest at least 2 hours, unrefrigerated.

Meanwhile, melt the butter in a heavy skillet over moderate heat. Sauté the ham bits until lightly browned. Remove them to a dish with a slotted spoon and keep them warm.

Pour the batter into a 4-cup measure. Reheat the skillet with its remaining butter until hot but not smoking. Pour one quarter of the batter (about ½ cup) into the skillet, sprinkle with one quarter of the ham, and bake until brown on the bottom. Turn and brown on the other side. Slide the cake onto an ovenproof dish and keep it warm in a 200° F. oven. Make 3 more pancakes in the same fashion, adding oil to the pan when necessary. Serve 1 cake to each person with Apple Cider Syrup or Cranberry Syrup (page 27).

VARIATION: In the Netherlands, this same batter is enriched with an extra egg and divided in half to make 2 giant pancakes. After sautéing the ham, one half the batter is poured into the skillet, sprinkled with half the ham bits, and browned on the bottom. Then it is slipped into an ovenproof dish, placed in a preheated 350° F. oven, and baked until the top is light golden, about 20 minutes. Meanwhile, the second pancake is made. The first is kept hot until the second is finished, and the two are sandwiched with butter and a sprinkling of sugar.

It is served cut in 4 wedges, with one of the suggested syrups.

APPLE CIDER SYRUP

~

2 quarts apple juice or
unpasteurized apple cider

In a 3-quart stainless steel pot or preserving kettle, bring the juice or cider to a boil over medium heat. Skim it frequently as it boils, until reduced to 1¼ or 1⅓ cups. Let it cool slightly and pour into a glass jar or pitcher. Serve warm. ~ This will make 1¼ to 1⅓ cups.

Sour Cream Pancakes

Just as chicken soup brings the reassuring warmth of childhood back to some people, when I first came back from living twenty-two years abroad, my son confessed that sour cream pancakes meant mother to him. Therefore, when giving my first cooking demonstration in New York at Bloomingdale's, I decided to use this recipe for its endorsed appeal. ～ It serves four.

½ cup sour cream
½ cup skim milk
2 large eggs, separated
¾ cup unbleached, all-purpose flour
1 teaspoon baking powder
1 tablespoon sugar
Salt to taste
½ cup butter, melted
Blueberry Syrup

Mix the sour cream and milk and pour over the egg yolks in a medium-size bowl; whisk together. Sift the flour together with the baking powder, sugar, and salt and whisk into the egg mixture by tablespoonfuls. Add the melted butter and stir until smooth.

Whisk the egg whites until stiff but not dry, and fold into the batter.

Over moderate heat, heat a griddle or skillet until a drop of water skates over the surface. Brush lightly with oil and drop the batter on by tablespoonfuls. When the first side is golden brown, turn and brown the other side. Keep warm in an ovenproof dish in a 200° F. oven.

Serve with Blueberry Syrup.

BLUEBERRY SYRUP

~

4 cups blueberries, rinsed
and drained

3 cups water

2 strips lemon peel

3 cups sugar

Lemon juice to taste

Put the blueberries in a saucepan and crush them with a potato masher or wooden spoon until most of the skins are broken. Add 1 cup of the water and the strips of lemon peel and bring to a simmer. Turn the heat to low and cook the berries for 5 minutes at just under a simmer.

Pour the berries into a strainer lined with 3 layers of cheesecloth and let the juice drip through. Twist the cloth to extract all the juice. There should be about 2 cups. Discard the berry pulp.

Combine the remaining 2 cups of water with the sugar in a small saucepan. Bring the mixture to a boil, stirring until the sugar is dissolved and the mixture is clear. Wash down the sides of the pan with a wet pastry brush. Boil the syrup without stirring until it reaches 260° F. on a candy thermometer.

Add the reserved blueberry juice and bring the mixture back to a boil. Boil for 1 minute. Let the syrup cool, then add a few drops of lemon juice to taste, according to the tartness of the berries.

Pour the syrup into two 1-pint jars and refrigerate if you plan to use it within a week or two (see page 13). ~ This recipe makes about 4 cups.

Oat Cakes

*I*n the coldest climates, oats have always been the preferred cereal, and today nutritional experts have confirmed that except for wheat germ, oats contain more protein than any other grain. ~ In ancient Scotland, the legendary Robert Bruce attributed his armies' successful maneuvers to their extreme mobility, since there were no cumbersome provision wagons to slow them down. Every man carried with him a sack of oats and an iron plate—instant oat cakes. If Napoleon's soldiers had been similarly equipped, think of the difference to his snowbound and starving Russian campaign troops! ~ These hearty breakfast pancakes must be started the night before. ~ The recipe is enough for six hungry appetites.

2 cups rolled (not quick-cooking) oats
2 cups buttermilk
½ cup unbleached, all-purpose flour
1 tablespoon sugar
1 teaspoon baking soda
3 large eggs, lightly beaten
3 tablespoons butter, melted

Combine the oats and buttermilk in a large bowl and put in a cool place to soak overnight.

Sift the flour, sugar, and baking soda together into another large bowl. Stir in the oats mixture. Add the eggs and melted butter and beat until thoroughly combined.

Heat a griddle or skillet until a drop of water dances on the surface. Brush with oil and drop the batter, 2 tablespoons at a time, or from a half-filled ¼-cup measure. Bake until browned on the bottom; turn to brown the other side. Serve immediately or keep warm in an ovenproof dish in a 200° F. oven. Top with plain yogurt flavored with orange juice concentrate.

Health-Nut Barley Cakes

N*o salt, no sugar—only a little honey—no cholesterol, no un-bleached or bleached flour, makes these raised cakes a splendid way to start the day. Almost everyone I know is on a low-fat diet, taking vitamins, eating foods with more fiber, etc.—even me.* ⌇ *Barley flour and soy milk powder can be found in health food stores or in the health food section of supermarkets.* ⌇ *This amount will serve four to five people.*

2   packages dried yeast
½   cup lukewarm water
1   tablespoon honey
3   large egg whites
1   cup barley flour
1   cup wheat germ
2   tablespoons vegetable oil
⅓   cup soy milk powder
½   cup skim milk powder
1   cup warm water
     Sugarless Applesauce (page 112)

Sprinkle the yeast over the ½ cup of water in a small bowl. Stir in the honey and let sit until light and bubbly, about 20 minutes.

In a large bowl, whisk the egg whites just until foamy and white, not stiff. Fold in the flour, then the wheat germ. Add the oil.

Whisk the milk powders into the cup of water, combining thoroughly. Stir into the flour mixture until blended.

Heat a griddle or skillet until a drop of water skates over the surface. Drop the batter from a full ¼-cup measure and brown on both sides. Brush the surface of the griddle with oil, only if needed. Keep the pancakes in an ovenproof dish in a 200° F. oven until all are made. Accompany with Sugarless Applesauce or honey.

Fluffy Dutch Pancakes

In Holland, after the Reformation, the pre-Lenten carnival, or ker-mis, was secularized into a village fair where stands erected along the canals sold doughnuts and griddle cakes. Some of the pancakes were iced with pink sugar and contained dried fruits, but most in demand were the poffertjes, *puffy pancakes that were eaten as fast as they could be made. ⌐ This makes four servings.*

> 3 large eggs, separated
> ¼ cup sugar
> 1 cup unbleached, all-purpose flour
> 1 teaspoon baking powder
> ½ teaspoon salt (optional)
> 4 tablespoons butter, melted and cooled
> ¾ cup milk
> Apricot preserves

In a large bowl, whisk the egg yolks with the sugar until pale and lemon colored. Into another bowl, sift the flour with the baking powder and the salt, if used. Stir in the melted butter. Mix these ingredients into the egg mixture alternately with the milk and stir until smooth.

Whisk the egg whites until stiff but not dry. Fold them into the batter until just combined. Do not beat the mixture.

Heat a skillet, 9 to 10 inches in diameter, over moderate heat until a drop of water dances on the surface. Pour in ¾ cup of batter and, when bubbles appear, turn with a flexible spatula. Cook until the underside is golden, about 4 minutes. Transfer to a heated plate and serve at once, spread with apricot preserves.

Child's Butter Cakes

hese raised pancakes are unique in that they are rolled out and cut with a biscuit cutter. I tried substituting ½ cup of whole-wheat flour for the same amount of all-purpose flour with delicious results, but even without this nutritious addition, these pancakes were proved rib-sticking by hungry hordes in the Child's restaurants of the thirties. ~ You will be able to serve four people amply.

2 packages dried yeast
1½ cups lukewarm water
1 teaspoon sugar
    Salt to taste
3½ cups unbleached, all-purpose flour
2 tablespoons softened butter
½ cup melted butter for serving

Sprinkle the yeast over ½ cup of the lukewarm water. Stir in the sugar and salt and let rest 10 minutes, or until it bubbles. Add ½ cup of flour and stir until smooth. Let rise 15 minutes.

Work in the rest of the flour alternately with the remaining 1 cup of water with a wooden spoon and then with your hands, until the dough leaves the sides of the bowl. Butter another large bowl with the softened butter and add the dough, turning it until all sides are coated. Cover with a cloth and let it rise in a warm place out of drafts until doubled in volume, about 1 hour.

Punch down the dough and turn it out onto a lightly floured surface. Roll it out ½-inch thick and cut it into 3-inch rounds.

Heat a griddle or skillet over medium heat until a drop of water skates over the surface. Cook the cakes until brown on the underside (this will take 4 to 5 minutes), then turn them with a spatula to brown the other side (about 3 to 4 minutes).

Serve at once with the melted butter, or split the cakes like English muffins and spread with butter. Apple jelly is perfect with them either way.

Raised Buckwheat Cakes

ven though you must begin the preparation for these pancakes the night before, it is more than worth the time when you smell the enchanting aroma that arises as they cook. I am willing to wager that no one will be able to sleep through the first pancake. You might improve the shining hour by serving them with Caramelized Apples. ~ *This recipe will feed six people.*

    1   package dried yeast
 2¼   cups lukewarm water
    1   tablespoon sugar
    2   cups buckwheat flour
    1   cup unbleached, all-purpose flour
    1   teaspoon salt (optional)
    3   tablespoons unsulfured molasses
        Caramelized Apples

In a large mixing bowl, dissolve the yeast in ¼ cup of the lukewarm water. Stir in the sugar and let stand until bubbly, about 10 minutes. In another bowl, combine the flours. Add the salt if desired. Stir the remaining 2 cups of water into the yeast mixture and whisk. Add the flour mixture and stir until smooth with a wooden spoon. Cover with a cloth and leave in a warm place, 78° F., overnight.

In the morning, stir down the batter and add the molasses. Heat the griddle until a drop of water skids over it. Brush with oil and try a tablespoonful of batter. It should spread to a thickness of ⅛ inch. If the batter is too thick to spread easily on the hot griddle, thin it with drops of lukewarm water. When the batter is the proper consistency, use a full ¼-cup measure for each cake. Cook until bubbles appear, then turn to brown the other side. Keep the finished cakes in an ovenproof dish in a 200° F. oven. Serve with the apples, or with melted butter and maple syrup or warmed honey.

CARAMELIZED APPLES

~

6 Golden Delicious apples
6 tablespoons (¾ stick) butter
⅓ cup sugar
   Nutmeg (optional)

Peel and core the apples and cut into ¼-inch slices. Melt the butter in a heavy skillet and sauté the apples with the sugar until the sugar begins to caramelize. The slices should be translucent but not lose their shape. Cover the buckwheat cakes with the warm apples and fold in quarters. If desired, sprinkle with a little nutmeg. ~ This serves 4.

Little Hoecakes

This is my updated version of an old southern recipe for the corncakes that were baked on the blade of a hoe over an open fire. The small rounds can be split like English muffins and crisped in the oven, or eaten whole with the healthful goodness of Yogurt Cheese. ⁓ Hoecakes keep very well in an airtight container. To reheat, they need only be sprinkled with a few drops of water and wrapped in foil. Place in a preheated 350° F. oven for 15 minutes and they taste newly baked. ⁓ This recipe makes about 24 2½-inch cakes.

1¼	cups unbleached, all-purpose flour
¼	cup white cornmeal
¼	teaspoon baking soda
¼	teaspoon salt (optional)
2½	tablespoons sugar
4	tablespoons chilled butter or margarine, cut in small bits
½	cup plain yogurt (the low-fat style may be used)
	Yogurt Cheese

Sift the dry ingredients into a medium-size bowl. Rub in the butter or margarine until evenly distributed. Add the yogurt and combine with your hands until a stiff dough is formed. Pat it into a ball and let it rest under a cloth for 30 minutes.

Divide the dough in half and roll each half on a lightly floured surface to a thickness of ¹⁄₁₆ inch. Cut out 2½-inch rounds.

When all the cakes have been cut, heat a griddle over low heat until a drop of water skates across it. Place the rounds on the ungreased griddle and cook 4 minutes on each side. The cakes will rise very slightly. Remove with a spatula to a baking sheet and keep warm in a 200°F. oven. Split them while warm and spread with Yogurt Cheese. If desired, the split halves may be arranged on a baking sheet and crisped in a 300° F. oven for 15 minutes.

YOGURT CHEESE

~

2 cups plain yogurt

Line a sieve or colander with 2 thicknesses of cheesecloth. Place over a smaller bowl so that the sieve does not touch the bottom of the bowl. Pour in the yogurt and let it drain overnight in the refrigerator. (The longer the yogurt drains, the firmer the cheese will be.)

In the morning, discard the liquid and let the cheese return to room temperature before using. ～ This will make about 1½ cups.

NOTE: An interesting snack spread can be made by stirring in 4 tablespoons of any fresh herb, such as tarragon, basil, or parsley, finely chopped. Never, *never* add salt.

Peter Rabbit Pancakes

I*n honor of my grandsons, Benjamin, Thibaud, and Zachary— with a curtsy on the side to Beatrix Potter—I recommend these deliciously crunchy pancakes to desperate mothers. Their name alone will open sleepy breakfasttime eyes. ⁓ Here I must remember to thank the food processor manufacturers because they make this kind of recipe so easy. Of course, it can be made by hand—grated on a hand grater, chopped with a knife, passed through a food mill—but in this instance I prefer the machine. ⁓ This amount makes eight to ten good-size pancakes, serving 4 or 5.*

  2 cups grated carrots, loosely packed (about 3 medium carrots)
  ½ cup unbleached, all-purpose flour
  2 eggs, well beaten
  ¼ cup milk
  ¼ teaspoon mace (optional)
  2 tablespoons vegetable oil
     Orange Hash

In a large bowl, mix the carrots and flour with a fork. Stir in the eggs and milk. Flavor with mace, if desired. Mix thoroughly.

Heat a griddle over moderate heat until a drop of water hisses on contact. Stir the oil into the batter, and using a full ¼-cup measure, drop the batter onto the griddle. Spread with the back of the measuring cup into 3- to 3½-inch rounds. When they are brown on the bottom, about 2 minutes, turn them to brown the other side. The cakes will be pleasingly shaggy in appearance. Keep them warm in a 200° F. oven until the remaining cakes are made.

Serve two pancakes to each person, with a scoop of Orange Hash on the side.

ORANGE HASH

~

2 seedless navel oranges

1 small eating apple

2 tablespoons honey

Cut the peel and pith off the oranges with a sharp knife. Remove the central pith and separate the fruit into sections. Drop into the food processor. Peel and core the apple, cut in chunks, and add to the orange sections. Pulse the food processor on and off until the apple is in tiny pieces and all the orange membrane has been chopped small. *Do not purée the fruit.*

Pour the mixture into a strainer placed over a bowl, reserving the liquid for another use. Place the hash in a small bowl and stir in the honey. Mix thoroughly. ~ This makes about 1 cup.

Savory
PANCAKES

Breakfast pancakes are traditional and comforting; dessert crêpes give an elegant, or a frivolous, flourish to the end of a dinner. Joyfully, however, there exists a world of savory dishes for the hours in between. In the United States, until recently, pancakes were considered breakfast food, but now we have learned from the rest of the world to eat them around the clock. ~ These savory recipes can be interchanged as first courses or entrées and many can serve equally well as accompaniment to a main dish at dinner. They are perfect as an after-theater supper or a midnight snack. ~ For the hour of the apéritif, pancakes can be transformed into the tidbits that the French call *amuse-gueules,* or mouth pleasers. The Sour Cream Pancake batter (page 30) or the Blini (page 76) can be made silver-dollar size, just big enough for a dot of *crème fraîche* and three or four grains of red or black caviar. ~ Crêpes are the most refined member of the pancake family, and the most versatile. There is basically just one batter, made with or without sugar depending on its place on the menu. Because crêpes are neutral, they marry with virtually every type of filling or sauce, sweet or savory. ~ Originally the crêpe was sweet; it was served at the end of a many-course dinner. Sometimes it was even the theme of a party. In the *Larousse Gastronomique,* which is to things culinary what *Webster's Dictionary* is to a scholar, the crêpe recipe calls for twelve eggs and more than a cup of sugar, making approximately four dozen crêpes for eight people! Today, when appetites are less robust than in the nineteenth century, the extra crêpes can be easily frozen for future pleasure. ⌒ The unsweetened crêpe, which came much later, is at the present time the more popular version. Besides its many delicious permutations, because of its lower caloric count, it is a welcome substitute for bread or other starch in a meal. ⌒ Crêpes can be formed in many different shapes for varied uses. They can be fitted into greased muffin pans or custard cups to make flowerlike containers for vegetables or mini-quiches, delightful to serve at a luncheon. Five-inch rectangles can be made by cutting off the curved sides of crêpes, and by halving these again, small rectangles are created, which can be rolled around sausage meat, small cocktail sausages, or slices of marinated chicken, for a cocktail bite. ⌒ Using a 2- to 2½-inch cookie cutter or other fancy shapes, you can make two or three canapé bases from each crêpe. Place them on a baking sheet in a preheated oven for five minutes and *voilà!* little hearts or diamonds or rounds, ready for any topping you desire. ⌒ Divided into wedges, a crêpe can be rolled around a medium-size shrimp to make a tiny croissant. These can be pinned with toothpicks to a pineapple for a spectacular presentation. Your imagination is the only tool needed to make new and pleasing combinations.

Basic Entrée Crêpes

*N*ext to the cash register in every French comestibles—*combination delicatessen and hot food takeout shop*—there is a stack of plastic-wrapped crêpes, with no preservatives, no refrigeration, ready to eat. To me, newly arrived from this country where "shelf life" is an important ingredient in all our food, it was a mystery. ⌇ When I had my own restaurant, I kept packages of homemade crêpes in my freezer, ready to create unplanned entrées and desserts against any sudden influx of impatient customers. This is my basic crêpe recipe, perfect for any number of fillings, some of which are on the following pages. ⌇ This will make 32 to 36 crêpes.

> 4 large eggs
> 2 cups unbleached, all-purpose flour
> 1 cup milk
> 1 cup water
> 4 tablespoons butter, melted
> Pinch of salt (optional)
> Vegetable oil for the griddle

Whisk the eggs and flour together by hand or in a food processor until well mixed. Gradually add the milk and water. Beat in the butter. Let the batter rest, covered, in a cool place or in the refrigerator for at least 1 hour. (Do not keep it longer than 10 hours, and *never* freeze the batter. It takes longer to defrost it than to make it from scratch.)

When the batter is ready to use, thin it with a little milk if necessary. It should pour like heavy cream.

Heat a crêpe pan over moderate heat, until a drop of water sizzles on contact. Brush lightly with vegetable oil and lift off the heat. With the other hand, half-fill a ¼-cup measure with batter and pour it into the pan. Immediately tilt and swirl the pan to spread the batter evenly over the surface in a thin film. Pour any excess batter back into the bowl and return the pan to the heat.

In about 1 minute the crêpe will be ready to turn. Lift the edge with a small spatula to be sure it is an even gold color underneath. The crêpe should move freely. When the first side is golden brown, flip the crêpe with your fingertips or a small spatula. The second side takes only ½ minute to cook and will be speckled with brown, not evenly colored; this is the side that will take the filling.

Turn your crêpe onto a plate or cookie sheet. You can stack up to 8 crêpes without putting wax paper between each crêpe. When the crêpes are cool, wrap each stack in plastic wrap and refrigerate up to 3 days. To freeze, the plastic-wrapped packages should be put in a freezer bag or container. Defrost them at room temperature and they will be easy to separate and use. They can be reheated, if desired—wrapped in foil, not plastic—in a steamer or in a preheated 300° F. oven for 10 minutes.

If the crêpes begin to stick at any point, remove the empty pan from the heat and let it cool completely. With coarse (kosher) salt, rub over the surface to remove any particles of batter. Brush the surface with oil and heat it slowly until very hot but not smoking. Remove from the heat and let it cool before beginning again.

VARIATION: HERBED CRÊPES. For a beautiful, spring-inspired crêpe, add to the Basic Crêpe recipe 1 cup of any firmly packed, chopped fresh herb, such as dill, chives, tarragon, basil, or parsley. Or substitute a leafy green vegetable, finely chopped, like watercress, kale, spinach, or scallions. To compensate for the extra volume, you must subtract ⅔ cup of flour from the total amount used. If there is no cheese in the filling you plan to serve with the crêpes, you might also add 4 tablespoons of grated Parmesan. Prepare the batter and cook the crêpes as above.

The Herbed Crêpes can be rolled and cut in thin ribbons to garnish a clear consommé. Or, folded over tablespoons of cottage cheese, they are a welcome accompaniment to a mixed salad.

Crêpes with Scrambled Eggs and Green Peas

n any season this is a welcome dish, light but satisfying, and with a salad and fruit dessert, these flavorful crêpes make a perfect winter luncheon for four people.

3 tablespoons butter
8 large eggs
½ cup heavy cream
  Salt and pepper to taste
⅓ cup frozen petite green peas
8 Basic Entrée Crêpes (page 46)
1 tablespoon fresh minced herb (tarragon, chives, or mint)

Preheat the oven to 350° F.

Melt the butter in the top of a double boiler over simmering water. Break the eggs into a small bowl, add the cream, and season to taste with salt and pepper. Beat until foamy and pour into the melted butter. Cook, stirring constantly, for 3 minutes. Add the peas and continue stirring 2 minutes or until creamy. (Do not overcook or the filling will be too dry.) Remove the top of the double boiler from the heat.

Brush lightly with oil an overproof dish that will hold 8 rolled crêpes snugly. Divide the eggs between the 8 crêpes and roll up, pressing lightly along the cylinder to spread the eggs evenly. Fit into the ovenproof dish. Brush the tops of the crêpe rolls with oil and place in the oven for 5 minutes or until the crêpes are warmed through. Sprinkle with the herbs.

Serve two crêpes to each person.

Crêpes with Chicken and Broccoli Stir Fry

P receded by a light soup or bouillon and accompanied by a white wine, this is a regal meal for four.

   2 whole boneless chicken breasts (about 1½ lbs), skinned
   ½ cup soy sauce
   ½ cup dry sherry
   1 large garlic clove, crushed
1½ cups broccoli flowerets
   ⅓ cup peanut oil
   4 tablespoons cornstarch mixed with ¼ cup water
   8 Basic Entrée Crêpes (page 46)

Cut the breasts in ½-inch cubes. In a medium bowl, combine the soy sauce, sherry, and garlic. Stir in the chicken, being careful to coat all the cubes. Refrigerate for 2 hours.

Meanwhile, bring 2 quarts of water to a boil in a large saucepan. Cook the broccoli pieces for 5 minutes or until barely tender. Drain, then plunge them into cold water to refresh. Drain again and set aside.

Remove the chicken from the marinade with a slotted spoon, reserving as much marinade as possible. Preheat the oven to 350° F.

Heat the oil in a heavy skillet or wok over moderately high heat for 1 minute. Add the chicken pieces and stir-fry 2 to 3 minutes to brown faintly. Whisk the cornstarch and water into the reserved marinade and pour it over the chicken. Stir constantly until the sauce is translucent, about 2 minutes. Remove the skillet from the heat and let it cool to room temperature. Stir in the broccoli.

Divide the mixture between the 8 crêpes, spreading it across the middle of each, and fold in half. Arrange the crêpes overlapping slightly in an ovenproof dish and place them in the oven for 10 minutes. Serve immediately, 2 crêpes per person.

Ham and Endive Filled Crêpes

A classical first course in France is endives wrapped in slices of ham, covered with a sauce Mornay, and baked. The bread crumb and grated cheese topping on these crêpes instead of the rich sauce seems lighter. ～ They make a good beginning for dinner for eight, or a main luncheon entrée for four people.

> 8 Belgian endives
> 2 shallots, minced
> 4 tablespoons butter
> 1 tablespoon lemon juice
> 8 Basic Entrée Crêpes (page 46)
> 8 slices cooked ham (about ¼ pound)
> 3 tablespoons heavy cream
> ½ cup soft bread crumbs
> 1 tablespoon butter, melted
> ¼ cup grated Cheddar cheese

Preheat the oven to 350° F.

Wipe the endives with a damp cloth and trim a thin slice off the root end. Arrange them in a nonmetal ovenproof dish, sprinkle with the shallots, and dot with the butter. Cover tightly and bake for 20 minutes. You should be able to pierce the endives with a sharp knife blade when done. Sprinkle with the lemon juice and let cool.

Cover each crêpe with a slice of ham, trimming the ham to fit. Place 1 endive on the edge of each crêpe. Stir the cream into the pan juices and spoon 1 teaspoon over each crêpe. Roll up and arrange the rolls in an ovenproof dish.

Increase the oven temperature to 375° F. In a small bowl, mix together the bread crumbs, melted butter, and grated cheese. Sprinkle over the crêpes and bake for 15 to 20 minutes. Serve piping hot.

Swiss Fondue Crêpes

*H*ere is a new twist for an old Swiss favorite. ~ It can be enjoyed as a luncheon dish for four people, with the rich Hollandaise Sauce, or makes twelve appetizer servings.

- 8 ounces (½ pound) Emmenthaler or Tilsit cheese, grated
- ½ cup dry white wine
- 2 teaspoons cornstarch
- 1 tablespoon Kirsch
  Freshly ground black pepper
- 12 Basic Entrée Crêpes (page 46)
  Hollandaise Sauce (optional)

Preheat the oven to 400° F.

In the top of a double boiler, combine the grated cheese, wine, cornstarch, and Kirsch. Place over simmering hot water and stir until the cheese is melted and mixed thoroughly with the other ingredients. Remove from the hot water. Mix in the pepper.

To assemble, spoon 1½ tablespoons of filling onto each crêpe and roll. Arrange each as filled in an ovenproof dish and bake 5 minutes. Serve immediately, with or without the Hollandaise Sauce.

HOLLANDAISE SAUCE
~

- 3 large egg yolks
- 2 tablespoons lemon juice
- ½ cup hot melted butter
  Salt and paprika (optional) to taste

Place the yolks and juice in a blender or food processor. Cover and pulse the motor on and off. Using the opening in the cover of the blender or the feed tube of the processor, turn the motor on and pour in the melted butter in a steady stream. As soon as the sauce thickens, stop the motor. Season and serve immediately. ~ This makes 1½ cups.

Crêpe Purses with
Curried Vegetables

These amusing little packages can be used as a vegetarian entrée or as a side dish for poached fish or chicken, and even as a first course. For a vegetarian luncheon, double the recipe and serve two crêpes to each person. The crêpes are tied with a blanched strip of scallion or leek and have the appearance of a purse or pouch. ~ This recipe serves six people.

3	medium carrots, finely diced
1½	cups broccoli flowerets
6	8-inch strips scallion or leek greens
2	tablespoons butter
1	small onion, minced
2	stalks celery, finely diced
1	teaspoon curry powder (more if desired)
3	tablespoon unbleached, all-purpose flour
1	cup chicken stock
1	cup cooked corn kernels
1	cup fresh or defrosted green peas
	Salt and pepper to taste
6	Basic Entrée Crêpes (page 46)
3	tablespoons butter, melted

In a large pot or kettle, bring 3 quarts of water to a boil. Drop the carrots into the water and blanch for 2 minutes. Remove them with a slotted spoon or strainer and drain in a colander. Drop in the broccoli and blanch for 3 minutes. Remove with the slotted spoon and drain in the colander. Drop in the scallion strips and blanch for 1 minute. Remove with the slotted spoon and drain on paper towels.

Melt the 2 tablespoons of butter in a small heavy saucepan over moderate heat. Sauté the onion and celery until soft but not brown, then stir in the curry powder. Mix thoroughly and add the flour. Let the mixture cook for 3 minutes, stirring constantly. Add the stock and whisk until the sauce thickens, about 10 minutes. Remove from the heat.

In a large bowl, combine the carrots, broccoli, corn, and peas. Pour the sauce over them and mix thoroughly. Season to taste with salt and pepper.

Butter a baking sheet and arrange the crêpes flat on it. Divide the vegetables among the crêpes, heaping them in the middle. Gather the edges of the crêpes together into a pouch and tie with a strip of scallion. You may refrigerate the pouches until needed.

Preheat the oven to 350° F. Brush the crêpe bundles with the melted butter and bake for 15 to 20 minutes, or until the edges are crisp and golden. Serve hot.

Tulip Cups with Corn Custard

ttractive presentations are almost as important today as the food being served. Perhaps it is an attempt to make the millions of overweight people in our nation (me among them) believe that less is more. These vegetable and custard-filled crêpes are a good way to begin. ~ Any blanched vegetable may be substituted for the corn in this recipe for six people.

2 large eggs plus 1 yolk
¾ cup milk or light cream
¾ cup corn kernels, cut from 2 ears of corn or defrosted
1 tablespoon grated onion mixed with 1 tablespoon cornstarch
  Salt and pepper to taste
12 Basic Entrée Crêpes (page 46)

Preheat the oven to 350° F.

In a medium bowl, whisk the eggs and milk together. Stir in the corn and the onion and cornstarch. Mix thoroughly and season to taste with salt and pepper.

Using a muffin pan (6- or 8-ounce size) or glass custard cups, brush 12 cups with melted butter or vegetable oil. Fit a crêpe into each. Ladle the corn custard mixture into the cups, stirring from the bottom of the bowl each time to distribute the corn evenly. Place the custard cups, if used, on a baking sheet. Bake for 15 to 20 minutes or until the custard is firm.

Remove the tulip crêpes from the muffin tins or custard cups with the tip of a blunt knife and serve warm or at room temperature, 2 per person.

Seafood Torta
~ Gâteau de Crêpes aux Fruits de Mer ~

S tacking the crêpes with the filling between the layers like a cake makes a different and attractive presentation, but this dish does strain the budget. The two stacks of 6 crêpes are each cut in four wedges. ~ For a luncheon main dish, each person should have two wedges. As a first course the torta will serve eight people.

         6 tablespoons butter
         3 tablespoons minced shallots
        ¾ cup shredded cooked crabmeat
        ¾ cup small cooked shrimp
         2 lobster tails, cooked and diced
        ¼ cup Vermouth
         5 tablespoons unbleached, all-purpose flour
      1¼ cups light cream
         1 cup fish stock or bottled clam juice
        ½ cup grated Cheddar cheese
        12 Basic Entrée Crêpes (page 46)

In a small skillet, melt 2 tablespoons of the butter and sauté the shallots until transparent. In a medium bowl, mix the seafoods and the sautéed shallots. Stir in the Vermouth. Keep hot over hot water.

In a heavy saucepan, melt the remaining 4 tablespoons of butter. Whisk in the flour and cook, stirring, for 1 minute. Whisking constantly, add the cream and fish stock. Let it thicken over low heat. Pour one half of the sauce over the seafood and mix well.

Stir the grated cheese into the remaining sauce over low heat until the cheese is melted. Remove from the heat and keep warm.

Spread the seafood mixture between the crêpes, making 2 stacks of 6 crêpes each. Cut each stack in 4 wedges and serve 1 or 2 to each person, spooning sauce over each portion.

A Spinach Pancake from Persia

~ Isfanakh Fatira ~

his is not really a spinach pancake, but a pancake of spinach! This recipe, from Greene on Greens *by Bert Greene, is a delightful treat for vegetarians and, having no flour, is low in calories. He suggests it for brunch with yogurt or sour cream. ~ In the Middle East, vegetables such as leeks, eggplant, or zucchini are cooked, mixed with eggs, and fried like this. They make an interesting side dish for lamb or fish, or even an appetizer before the meal. ~ This amount serves two or three persons. It is better to make one recipe, or one skilletful, at a time, rather than doubling the recipe.*

4 tablespoons unsalted butter, melted
4 scallions, bulbs and green tops chopped
¼ cup chopped parsley
½ pound fresh spinach, washed and chopped
3 large eggs
   Pinch of salt
   Freshly ground black pepper

Melt 3 tablespoons of the butter in a skillet over medium heat and cook the scallions and parsley for 2 minutes, stirring constantly. Add the spinach and cook, covered, until the spinach begins to wilt, about 2 minutes. Uncover and cook 20 minutes, stirring occasionally. Let it cool.

In a large bowl, beat the eggs until light colored. Add the spinach mixture and combine thoroughly; season to taste with salt and pepper.

Melt the remaining tablespoon of butter in the skillet over medium heat. When hot, pour in all the batter at once and cover. Cook for 10 minutes. Loosen the edges with a spatula and turn it out on a serving plate. Cut in wedges to serve.

Plantain Pancakes

~ *Arepitas* ~

lantains, a close relative of the banana, are a common sight in our supermarkets despite their Latin American origin. They taste different when tree-ripened, but since they are cooked twice in this recipe their ripeness is less important. However, they should not be bright green or unresisting to the touch, but a pleasant dull green mottled with golden brown. This dish is not sweet and is perfect as a snack or accompaniment. ~ It serves four.

1 pound plantains (about 2–3 large)
¾ cup unbleached, all-purpose flour
1 teaspoon baking powder
½ teaspoon cinnamon
2 large eggs, separated
1 tablespoon brown sugar
1 cup milk
2 tablespoons butter, melted

Peel the plantains and cut them into small pieces. Drop them into boiling water to cover and cook over moderate heat for 10 minutes; drain. While hot, mash them or purée in a food processor. Let them cool. There should be about 1 cup of pulp.

Sift together the flour, baking powder, and cinnamon and combine with the plantain pulp. Beat in the egg yolks and sugar and add the milk.

In another bowl, whisk the egg whites until stiff but not dry. Fold the whites and the butter into the batter.

Heat a griddle until a drop of water sizzles on the surface. Brush it lightly with butter and drop the batter by tablespoonfuls. Brown on both sides and serve with butter and guava jelly, or unsweetened crushed pineapple.

Eggplant Pancakes with Pine Nuts

editerranean cooks dote on the eggplant—not only a marvelous substitute for meat, but beautiful to the eye and mineral-rich to the body—although I'm sure they would prefer it even without its healthful properties. I grew up on my mother's fried eggplant—round slices, crisp and golden, and disastrous for cholesterol counters. These cakes avoid that dire total and, served with Fresh Tomato Sauce, are a satisfying dish all year round. ⁓ *This recipe makes twelve to fifteen 3-inch cakes and will serve four or five people.*

1 medium eggplant, about ¾ pound
¼ cup pine nuts
2 medium eggs
½ cup unbleached, all-purpose flour
1 tablespoon vegetable oil
  Juice of 1 lemon
1 large garlic clove, crushed
1 small white onion, coarsely chopped
¼ teaspoon salt or to taste
¼ teaspoon freshly ground black pepper or to taste
  Fresh Tomato Sauce

Preheat the oven to 350° F.

Split the eggplant in two and place on a cookie sheet, cut surfaces up. Bake for 45 minutes or until very soft when pressed with the back of a spoon. Meanwhile, spread the pine nuts in a pie plate and place in the oven for 15 minutes or until golden. Set aside to cool. Remove the eggplant and while still very warm, scrape the pulp out of the skin with a spoon, working toward the stem end. Place the pulp in a blender or the bowl of a food processor.

In a medium bowl, beat the eggs into the flour. Mix in the oil and lemon juice. Stir in the garlic and onion. Add the mixture to the eggplant pulp and purée, stopping once or twice to scrape the sides with a rubber spatula. When smooth, turn the purée into a bowl. Fold in the pine nuts and season to taste with salt and pepper.

Heat a griddle over moderate heat until a drop of water rolls over the surface. If it sizzles and evaporates, the griddle is too hot. Lower the heat and drop the batter by heaping tablespoonfuls. Avoid the center of the griddle as it is the hottest spot. Spread each tablespoonful with the back of the spoon into a 3-inch cake. Lower the heat once again if the batter is difficult to spread, and grease the griddle after each batch. Cook until the underside is mottled with a dark golden crust, about 3 minutes. Turn with a pancake turner, pressing down lightly upon the cake. Cook until the second side is crusted, about 2 minutes. Remove to a cookie sheet and keep warm in a 200° F. oven. Do not stack the cakes.

Serve 2 or 3 to a person with the Fresh Tomato Sauce or a purée of spinach.

FRESH TOMATO SAUCE
~

10 tomatoes (about 2½ pounds)
3 tablespoons vegetable oil
1 medium onion, minced
3 garlic cloves, crushed
½ teaspoon dried thyme leaves
½ cup fresh coriander, basil, or
    tarragon leaves, chopped fine

Bring a large pot of water to a boil. Dip the tomatoes in the boiling water and slip off the skins. Cut the tomatoes in half and squeeze out the seeds and juice. Chop the pulp into small dice.

In a heavy saucepan, heat the oil and sauté the onion and garlic until softened. Add the tomatoes and herbs and simmer over moderate heat until the liquid has evaporated, about 20 to 25 minutes. Stir occasionally to prevent sticking. Remove from the heat and serve at room temperature. ~ This recipe makes about 2½ cups.

Zucchini Pancakes

*Z*ucchini, like spinach and broccoli, is always with us, and provides a green note in the middle of the grayest winter. It is so easy to grow that my neighbors and I have agreed that only one of us will plant it each year, and keep the others bountifully supplied. ~ In our desperate search for new ways to put it before our families, I invented this pancake, which serves six people.

2 pounds small zucchini
1 tablespoon salt
3 large eggs
6 tablespoons wheat germ or fine dried bread crumbs
1 teaspoon dried oregano, crushed fine
3 tablespoons vegetable oil
   Avgolemono Sauce

Wash the zucchini and dry with paper towels. Cut off both ends and discard. Grate the zucchini coarsely, with a food processor or by hand, and toss it together with the salt; place in a colander. Let it drain for 30 minutes, pushing down on the pulp from time to time. Discard all the liquid. A handful at a time, squeeze the pulp and place it in a medium bowl. It should be as dry as possible.

Beat in the eggs, then the wheat germ or crumbs. Stir in the oregano and oil and mix thoroughly.

Heat a crêpe pan or small heavy skillet over moderate heat until a drop of water skates over the surface. Using a ½-cup measure, spread the batter evenly in the pan. When the underside is firm and golden, turn it with a broad spatula and brown the other side. Keep the cakes warm in a 200° F. oven, arranged side by side on a baking sheet. Serve 2 pancakes to each person, passing the sauce separately.

AVGOLEMONO SAUCE

~

1 tablespoon butter

1 tablespoon unbleached,
   all-purpose flour

1 cup chicken broth

2 large eggs

   Juice of 2 large lemons

   Salt and pepper to taste

Melt the butter in the top of a double boiler over moderate
heat. Mix in the flour with a whisk, then add the broth and whisk for
3 minutes. Reduce the heat and simmer for 3 more minutes.

In a small bowl, beat the eggs until frothy. Beat in about one
third of the hot sauce, then return this mixture to the sauce
remaining in the double boiler top. Cook over simmering water,
stirring frequently, until the mixture thickens. Add the lemon juice
and continue cooking until the sauce is thick and creamy. Do not let
the water in the bottom of the double boiler come to a full boil.
Season the sauce with salt and pepper and serve. You can keep the
sauce warm for 30 minutes over the hot water, if necessary.

~ This makes about 1¼ cups.

Mark's Shrimp and Spinach Pancakes

*I*n my friend Mark's restaurant, Punchinello, these are a favorite luncheon specialty. The nutmeg and salt may be replaced by any fresh herb, finely minced. Chard (the green part only) may replace the spinach. The pancakes may also be frozen and reheated. Sautéed fresh corn kernels make a pretty accompaniment. ~ The recipe makes about twelve small pancakes, or four servings of three per person.

> 4 ounces spinach or chard, cooked and minced
> 4 ounces small shrimp, cooked and coarsely chopped
> 4 large eggs
> ¾ cup milk
> 2½ cups unbleached, all-purpose flour
> Salt, pepper, and nutmeg to taste

In a large bowl, thoroughly mix the spinach and shrimp. Beat in the eggs, then the milk. With a wooden spoon, stir in the flour and beat well. Season to taste and set aside, covered, for 30 minutes.

Heat a griddle or large skillet until a drop of water sizzles on contact, and brush lightly with butter. Using ¼ cup of batter for each, make the pancakes and brown them on both sides. Keep them warm in an ovenproof dish until ready to serve.

Roquefort-Filled Herbed Crêpes

T he colors of these crêpes are those of spring and summer, the perfect time for serving them. ～ The recipe that follows is enough for eight herbed crêpes, two to each of four people as a first course. If you wish to eliminate the cream topping, each crêpe, heated and cut in four, can be served as an appetizer with drinks before dinner.

> 8 ounces Roquefort or any blue cheese
> 6 tablespoons unsalted butter
> 3 tablespoons unbleached, all-purpose flour
> 8 Herbed Crêpes (page 47)
> ½ cup heavy cream or *crème fraîche* (see Note)

In a small bowl, mash the cheese with the butter into a paste. Add the flour and mix thoroughly.

On a floured surface, form the mixture into a long roll, 1 inch in diameter. Refrigerate for 1 hour or until the roll is very firm.

Heat the oven to 375° F.

Cut the roll into 8 parts. Place 1 part on the lower edge of each crêpe. Press the cheese mixture lightly, extending it to the sides of the crêpe. Roll into a cylinder and arrange in a lightly oiled ovenproof dish.

Spread the cream over the rolls, and bake for 15 to 20 minutes, or until golden.

NOTE: *Crème fraîche* is costly to buy but easy to make at home. Simply stir ½ cup of sour cream into 1 cup of heavy cream. Let the mixture stand at room temperature in a glass container, covered lightly with a cloth, overnight. Refrigerate for 10 days or more. (It will continue to thicken in the refrigerator.)

Tex-Mex Pancakes

To me, *these are pure Texas—or, I should say, Laredo—where avocados growing in backyards ripen until they can be spooned out of the skin without mashing. Although the Mexicans use pinto beans to make their refried beans, which is what this pancake really is, I prefer overcooked kidney beans. ⁓ Serve it forth with guacamole to four people. This recipe requires advance preparation.*

  ½ pound dried kidney (red) beans
  4 tablespoons lard or vegetable shortening
  1 large onion, minced
  1 tablespoon red wine vinegar *or* 3 tablespoons red wine
  2 egg yolks, beaten
  1 teaspoon ground cumin
     Guacamole

Soak the beans in water to cover by a depth of 2 inches, overnight or for at least 6 hours. Drain and place them in a large saucepan, covering with fresh water to the same depth. Bring them to a boil over medium heat; drain again. Return the beans to the pot, cover with boiling water, and simmer over moderate heat until they are very soft and bursting, adding boiling water as needed. Remove from the heat.

Melt 2 tablespoons of the shortening in a heavy skillet and cook the onion just until soft. Stir it into the beans and purée the mixture in a food processor or food mill.

Stir the vinegar into the beans. (If using wine, bring it to a boil in a small enameled or stainless steel saucepan and cook until it is reduced to 1 tablespoon.) Mix the yolks and the cumin into the bean mixture.

Heat a griddle until a drop of water sizzles on the surface. Brush it with the remaining shortening and drop the batter by tablespoonfuls. Brown the cakes on both sides and keep them warm on a baking sheet, without stacking, in a 200° F. oven.

Put 2 or 3 pancakes on each of 4 warmed plates. Top each serving with 2 tablespoons of Guacamole and pass the rest separately.

GUACAMOLE
~

2   ripe tomatoes

½   cup cilantro leaves (fresh coriander), finely chopped

1   medium white onion, grated

2   garlic cloves, crushed and minced

¼   cup fresh lime juice

2   or 3 jalapeño peppers, or to taste

3   ripe avocados

In a bowl, pour boiling water over the tomatoes. Let stand 30 seconds and drain. Slip off the skins and cut the tomatoes in half. Squeeze out the seeds and chop coarsely. Squeeze out the remaining juice and discard or reserve for another use. Transfer to a bowl and stir in the cilantro, onion, garlic, and lime juice.

Chop the jalapeño peppers finely, being careful to wash your hands afterward to avoid burns. Stir the peppers into the tomato mixture.

When ready to serve, mash the avocados coarsely with a fork or potato masher (do not purée) and fold them into the tomato mixture. Cover the surface of the Guacamole with plastic wrap between servings to prevent it from darkening. ~ This will make about 1½ cups.

Corn Crêpes

This is an old southern recipe that is very versatile: cooked in a skillet, they are like fancy hush puppies and are a good partner for baked ham. Cooked in a crêpe pan, they make pancakes that can be folded around a filling and served as a main dish for lunch or a late supper. Corn crêpes are equally appropriate as a first course. ~ The spinach and ricotta filling used for Crespolini (page 68) is also delicious with this recipe, which is ample for five or six people.

- 2 cups white cornmeal
- ½ teaspoon baking soda
- 1 teaspoon baking powder
- 3 tablespoons unbleached, all-purpose flour
- 1 teaspoon salt (optional)
- 3 tablespoons minced onion or scallions
- 1 cup buttermilk
- 1 large egg, lightly beaten
- 1 cup corn kernels, fresh or frozen (optional)
- ½ cup vegetable oil
  Pumpkin Filling
- 3 tablespoons melted butter
- ¼ cup grated Parmesan cheese

Sift the dry ingredients, including the salt, if desired, into a large bowl. Stir in the onion, buttermilk, and egg. Fold in the corn, if desired.

Heat a crêpe pan, until a drop of water skips on the surface, and brush with the oil. Lift the pan off the heat and, using a full ¼-cup measure, pour in the batter. Swirl the pan to spread the batter evenly. Return to the heat and cook until the cake is golden on both sides. They may be stacked and kept warm in an ovenproof dish in a 200° F. oven.

Preheat the oven to 400° F.

Spread 1 heaping tablespoon of Pumpkin Filling on half of each pancake. Fold the other half over the filling and arrange in an ovenproof dish, overlapping the crêpes. Brush them with melted butter, sprinkle with grated cheese, and bake until the cheese is melted, 8 to 10 minutes.

VARIATION: To make corn cakes, heat 2 tablespoons of oil in a heavy skillet until hot but not smoking. Drop the batter by heaping tablespoonfuls and fry until golden on both sides. Drain on paper towels.

PUMPKIN FILLING

2   tablespoons butter

4   tablespoons minced shallots

1½   cups pumpkin purée

½   cup Ricotta cheese

4   tablespoons minced scallions

¼   cup grated Parmesan cheese

Melt the butter in a skillet and cook the shallots until soft. Add the pumpkin purée and cook over low heat until it is heated through. Remove from the heat and transfer to a bowl. Mix thoroughly with the Ricotta, scallions, and Parmesan.

Crespolini

O ne day, the editor of Corriere della Sera, the famous Italian newspaper, was coming to lunch in my Parisian kitchen on the Boulevard Malesherbes. It was my favorite room of the immense apartment: the exact dimensions of the three-car garage underneath, floored with old red tiles, walls and 14-foot ceiling papered in a Persian chintz pattern, and with a fireplace to offset the chill that rose from the garage below. ~ To show off my knowledge of northern Italian cuisine, I had planned a menu beginning with Crespolini, delicate crêpes enfolding Ricotta and spinach, hidden beneath a golden, bubbling sauce. I produced the dish with pride, remembering the afternoon spent in a sweltering Milanese kitchen learning how to make it. My guest leaped to his feet after a forkful. Raising his wineglass to me, he cried, "A triumph of French cuisine!" How was I to know that he was from Calabria—southern Italy? ~ This serves four or five people.

     2 large eggs
     ½ cup milk
     ¼ cup water
     ¾ cup plus 2 tablespoons unbleached, all-purpose flour
     1 tablespoon vegetable oil
        Salt to taste

FILLING
     1 10-ounce package frozen, chopped spinach, defrosted
     1 cup Ricotta cheese
     1 large egg
     6 tablespoons grated Parmesan cheese
     4 tablespoons butter
     4 tablespoons minced shallots
     4 tablespoons grated Mozzarella cheese
     ¼ cup crème fraîche (page 63)

In a medium bowl, whisk together the eggs, milk, and water. Whisk in the flour and add the oil and the salt, if desired. Let the batter rest for 2 hours, covered with a cloth, at room temperature.

Heat a crêpe pan until a drop of water sizzles on the surface. Half-fill a ¼-cup measure with batter, and holding the pan off the heat, pour in the batter, swirling the pan to spread the batter evenly. Pour any excess batter back into the bowl. In less than a minute the crêpe will be golden brown on the bottom. Flip and brown the other side and slide the crêpe onto a cookie sheet. Stack the crêpes as they are done; there will be 8 to 10. Cover them with a cloth until ready to fill.

To make the filling, drain the spinach in a sieve and squeeze out all the moisture. In a large bowl, mix the spinach and Ricotta. Add the egg and 4 tablespoons of Parmesan. Blend thoroughly and set aside.

In 2 tablespoons of the butter, sauté the shallots until transparent. Let them cool and add them to the spinach mixture.

To assemble the Crespolini, preheat the oven to 375° F. Spread a generous tablespoon of filling on the bottom third of each crêpe, and roll up. Cut each into three triangular pieces.

Mix the remaining 2 tablespoons of Parmesan with the Mozzarella. Spread each of 4 or 5 ramekins with 1 tablespoon of *crème fraîche.*

Arrange 5 or 6 sections of crêpes on the *crème fraîche* in each ramekin and dot 1 teaspoon of *crème fraîche* on each section. Sprinkle the cheese mixture over each serving and dot with the remaining butter. Bake for 20 minutes or until cheese is melted and golden.

Serve hot as a first course. As a luncheon entrée, accompany with a green salad.

Filigreed Crêpes with Caviar

This is a little fantasy from Judith Olney's book Summer Food. *Perhaps I should call it a folly since she invented it to be served with caviar. She also claims that it is enough for four persons —never! It is barely sufficient for me and one other appreciative guest. ~ To serve two to each of four people, you must double the recipe.*

 2 tablespoons unbleached, all-purpose flour
   Salt to taste
 1 large egg
 1 tablespoon clarified butter (page 101)
 ½ cup lukewarm milk
 ½ cup *crème fraîche* (page 63)
 4 ounces caviar (the best you can afford)
   Chopped dill (optional)
 4 lemon slices, notched and twisted

Sift the flour with the salt, if used. In a medium bowl, whisk the egg and butter together, then beat in the flour. Whisk in the milk. Let it rest for 1 hour.

Heat a crêpe pan until hot enough to make a drop of water bounce in the pan. Lift the pan off the heat, and with the other hand, pour in 1 tablespoon of batter, swirling the pan to spread it. Flip the crêpe when golden on the bottom and cook the other side. Make 4 crêpes and stack them as finished.

Now, lifting the pan again, dip a fork in the batter and loop it over the surface of the pan, making a lacy pattern. Return to the heat and cook quickly. It may not be necessary to flip the crêpe if it is filigreed enough. Continue with the rest of the batter, laying each lacy crêpe individually on a cloth. Spread each solid crêpe with *crème fraîche* and cover with the precious gray (or black or red) pearls. Top with the lacy crêpe and serve on a beautiful plate, garnished with dill, if desired, and lemon slices.

Omelet Crêpes with Asparagus

T hese crêpes spell springtime to me. Of course, asparagus is now available all year round, but it will never taste as new and special as it did when I had to wait through the cold months for its first appearance. ~ This makes two apiece for four people.

½ cup unbleached, all-purpose flour

6 large eggs

1½ cups heavy cream

¼ teaspoon white pepper

½ cup minced chives

24 thin asparagus spears

4 tablespoons butter

¼ cup grated Parmesan cheese

¼ cup grated Gruyère cheese

Place the flour in a large bowl and beat in the eggs one at a time. Still beating, add the cream. When combined, strain into another bowl and fold in the chives and pepper. Let the batter rest 1 hour or more in a cool place.

While the batter is resting, preheat the broiler. Trim the asparagus spears to 6 inches. Bring a large pot of water to a boil and drop in the asparagus just to blanch and brighten. After 30 seconds, remove the spears from the water with a wire strainer.

Heat a crêpe pan until a drop of water sizzles on the surface. Lift off the heat and pour in ¼ cup of the batter, stirring to distribute the chives before each use. Cook the crêpe over medium heat until set, about 2 minutes. Turn it to cook the other side. Keep the crêpes in an ovenproof dish in a 200° F. oven until all are made.

Lay 3 asparagus spears on the lower third of each crêpe, dot with butter, and roll. Arrange them side by side in an ovenproof dish and sprinkle with the two cheeses. Slide under the broiler, 6 inches from the heat, just long enough to soften the cheese.

Red Pepper Pancakes

Every year the practitioners of Nouvelle Cuisine discover a new food. It doesn't have to be one unknown until then, but one that had not figured prominently before. Last year was the Year of the Red Pepper, following the Year of the Coriander. ～ This recipe was invented by Jonathan Waxman, whose restaurant, Jam's, is one of the best of the New American Cuisine temples. ～ Even though the recipe, with its two kinds of caviar, is extravagant, it is a show stopper as a first course for four people.

        2 large sweet red peppers
        1 ear of corn
        1 tablespoon olive oil
        2 tablespoons butter
        1 shallot, minced
        1 cup heavy cream
     1½ cups unbleached, all-purpose flour
        1 tablespoon baking powder
        1 teaspoon salt (optional)
        1 cup milk
        3 large eggs, separated
           Olive oil for the griddle
        2 ounces Osetra caviar
        2 ounces red caviar
        2 tablespoons chopped chives
        2 tablespoons cilantro (coriander)

Roast the peppers over a flame or under a broiler, turning to blacken all sides. Remove the charred skin, stems, and seeds under cold running water. Dice 1 pepper very fine and set it aside. Cut the second pepper in half lengthwise; cut one half in fine julienne strips and mince the other almost to a purée. Set aside.

Remove the kernels from the ear of corn with a sharp knife. Sauté in a skillet in the olive oil and butter. After 3 minutes, add the diced pepper, the julienned strips of pepper, and the shallot. Cook for 2 minutes over medium heat, then stir in the cream. Simmer for 15 minutes and set aside.

Sift the flour, baking powder, and salt, if desired, into a bowl. Whisk in the milk and egg yolks and combine thoroughly. In another bowl, whisk the egg whites to form soft peaks and fold them into the yolk mixture. Fold in the reserved minced pepper.

Heat a griddle over medium heat until hot enough to make a drop of water sizzle. Grease it with olive oil and, using a half-filled ¼-cup measure, drop the batter onto the griddle. This will make cakes of approximately 3 inches in diameter. Brown them on both sides and keep them warm in an ovenproof dish in a 200° F. oven.

Warm 4 serving plates and make a small pool of red pepper sauce on each one. Overlap 2 pancakes on the sauce. Sprinkle with equal amounts of the two caviars, chives, and coriander leaves. Serve at once—to applause.

Paprika Pancakes
~ *Palascintà Paprikas* ~

*L*a Puszta is a real Hungarian inn in the fields outside Versailles, owned and run by a Hungarian couple who say the valley of the Chevreuse is reminiscent of their homeland. I was sous-chef there for a six-week "stage." ~ Sundays were the busiest days, and the most popular first course was the veal-stuffed crêpe in a paprika sauce. In the course of making these by the dozens, I became skillful at making crêpes and could manipulate three pans at a time on the eight-foot-long woodburning stove. ~ This recipe makes about twenty crêpes, or enough for six to eight people.

    1¼ cups all-purpose, unbleached flour
     1 teaspoon sugar
     1 cup milk
     4 large eggs
     1 cup seltzer or other carbonated water
       Butter for griddle

VEAL FILLING
     4 tablespoons butter
     1 large onion, chopped fine
     1 pound lean veal
    ¾ cup sour cream
     1 teaspoon salt (optional)
    ½ teaspoon cayenne or hot paprika
     1 tablespoon mild paprika

SAUCE
1¼ cups sour cream
     2 tablespoons cornstarch or potato flour
     1 tablespoon paprika (mild or hot, according to taste)

Place the flour, sugar, milk, and eggs in a large bowl and whisk until smooth and without lumps. Let it stand for 2 to 3 hours, covered, at room temperature.

When ready to cook the cakes, beat in the seltzer water. Heat a crêpe pan over moderate heat until a drop of water sizzles on the surface. Brush with butter, and using a half-filled ¼-cup measure, pour in the batter while holding the pan off the heat. Swirl the pan to spread the batter evenly, pouring any excess back into the bowl. When bubbles appear, turn the cake to lightly brown the other side. Stack the pancakes until all are made.

To make the filling, melt 1 tablespoon of butter in a heavy saucepan and cook the onion until transparent. Remove with a slotted spoon and set aside.

Cut the veal into ½-inch cubes. Melt the rest of the butter in the saucepan and add the veal. Over high heat, brown the veal pieces, turning the meat with a wooden spoon to brown all the sides. Remove with a slotted spoon to the onion dish.

Lower the heat and stir the sour cream into the pan juices, scraping to gather all the brown bits. Add the seasonings and stir until smooth. Return the veal and onions to the pan, and cover tightly. Simmer over low heat for 30 to 40 minutes or until the meat is tender enough to fall apart when pierced with a fork. During the cooking, check from time to time to make sure the meat is not sticking to the pan. Remove from the heat and cool, uncovered.

To make the sauce, mix the sauce ingredients together in a small heavy saucepan and cook over low heat, covered, until thick, about 20 minutes.

To assemble, preheat the oven to 350° F. Place 2 tablespoons of the veal mixture at one edge of each pancake. Fold in the two sides and roll up from the bottom. Place them in an ovenproof dish, cover with the sauce, and bake for 20 minutes or until the sauce begins to brown.

NOTE: At La Puszta, the rolled-up pancakes were chilled, then deep-fried and served with sauce spooned over each.

Elegant Blini with Smoked Salmon

I t was a lifetime ago that I feasted on blini and caviar for the first time at the Auberge d'Armaille in Paris. Then, a generation later, the ebullient Régine took over the restaurant, changed the name to the Maisonette Russe, and employed the equally effervescent Michel Guérard to update the cuisine. How do you update perfection? ~ Needless to say, the blini remained the same—heavenly. To maintain the luxurious note, they should be served with smoked salmon— for each person, two ounces of translucent, rosy slices, carelessly heaped like crumpled silk in the center of a circle of blini on each warm plate. ~ This makes four generous servings.

½ package dried yeast
¼ cup lukewarm water
   Pinch of salt
   Pinch of sugar
1 cup unbleached, all-purpose flour
3 large eggs, separated
1 cup milk, at room temperature
4 tablespoons butter, melted
8 ounces smoked salmon, sliced very thin

In a small bowl, stir the yeast into the water with the salt and sugar. Let it sit for 10 minutes or until foamy. Sift the flour into a medium bowl, make a well in the center, and mix in the egg yolks, one at a time, with a fork or your fingers. Add the milk slowly, whisking until smooth. Stir in the yeast mixture. Let it rest, covered with a cloth, in a warm place for 2 hours.

Whisk the egg whites until soft peaks are formed, and fold them into the batter. Let it rest for 15 minutes. Just before cooking the blini, gently fold in the melted butter.

Heat a griddle over moderate heat until a drop of water skates over the surface. Brush with more melted butter and drop the batter by tablespoonfuls. When the undersides are pale gold, turn and cook the other side, about 3 minutes in all. They should *not* be brown. If not serving one person at a time as each batch is finished (the other guests can sip their champagne and watch), keep the blini hot in a 200° F. oven on an ovenproof platter. Brush the griddle with melted butter between each series of blini.

Serve the blini on heated plates, surrounding a mound of salmon slices.

Dessert
PANCAKES

From the fragile hummingbird to the honey-loving grizzly, everything in nature has a sweet tooth, and man is no exception. Sweetness is a taste that does not have to be acquired. My twin grandsons, raised until the age of four without sugar of any kind except dried fruit, on first savoring ordinary hard candy —smuggled into their Christmas stockings by a wicked grandmother—became instant gourmands. ~ In the time-honored tradition, one saves the best for the last. With the knowledge that Chocolate Chocolate Hot Cakes or Peanut Butter Pancakes are waiting at the meal's end, the most fervent vegetable hater can eat his squash or spinach. ~ Because of their rich fillings and garnishes, dessert crêpes are purposely lighter than the basic entrée crêpes, but they are made in the same way. They can be eaten, as in nineteenth-century France, by the dozen, simply sprinkled with sugar, or folded around fruit or a sumptuous soufflé. Souffléed crêpes are impressive and imposing to see but very simple to make. ~ Since crêpes can be stored in the freezer for weeks at a time, the most elegant desserts are possible in a turn of the hand.

Basic Dessert Crêpes

From an old cookbook called La Cuisine Messine, *meaning the cooking of Metz, a city of Alsace-Lorraine in France, I have resurrected this recipe. The author, de Lazarque, quotes his countryman Anatole France: "Crêpes are an integral part of every family life . . . no good fête without them." ~ De Lazarque also said that crêpes should be as transparent as fine silk with edges like lace and always be accompanied by a glass of white wine. I prefer champagne, but the choice is yours. ~ This recipe makes twenty-four to thirty thin crêpes.*

> 1 cup plus 2 tablespoons unbleached, all-purpose flour
> 6 large eggs
> 1⅓ cups milk
> 3 tablespoons rum or Cognac
> 6 tablespoons unsalted butter, melted and cooled

Sift the flour into a large bowl. Whisk in the eggs, 2 at a time, and then the milk, one third at a time. Beat until smooth and pass through a fine sieve. Whisk in the rum or Cognac and let the batter rest, covered, for 1 hour in a cool place.

When ready to make the crêpes, whisk in 3 tablespoons of the melted butter. Heat a crêpe pan over moderate heat until a drop of water sizzles on contact with surface. Brush lightly with the remaining melted butter and lift the pan off the heat. With the other hand, half-fill a ¼-cup measure with batter and pour it into the pan. Tilt and swirl the pan to spread the batter evenly, pouring the excess back into the bowl. Return the pan to the heat and cook about 1 minute, when the crêpe can be easily flipped with your fingers or a small spatula. Brown the other side, a matter of seconds only, and slide the crêpe out onto a cookie sheet lined with a cloth. Make stacks of 6 crêpes until all the batter is cooked. Any unused crêpes may be wrapped in plastic wrap and refrigerated for a week or frozen (see page 47).

Sugared Buckwheat Crêpes
~ Galettes de Sarrasin ~

*I*n Brittany, which is the northwestern corner of France, these buckwheat pancakes are everywhere. They are thin as crêpes but 8 to 9 inches in diameter, and are eaten at any time from early morning to late night. They are sold from little stalls in the streets or in little restaurants called crêperies. In the street, they are handed to you, hot and sprinkled with sugar, folded in four. In the small crêperies, they can be had wrapped around sausages or ham or cheese, and are consumed in a more dignified way with a fork. ~ This recipe makes about ten large crêpes, four or five servings.

        1   cup buckwheat flour
     1½   cups unbleached, all-purpose flour
        ½   teaspoon salt
        2   cups milk
     1½   cups water
        5   large eggs, lightly beaten
        4   tablespoons butter, melted
            Approximately ¼ cup sugar

In a bowl or food processor, combine the flours and salt. In another bowl, whisk together the milk, water, and eggs. Whisk or process into the flour mixture in batches if necessary. Mix in the butter until smooth. Let stand 1 hour, covered with a cloth.

Heat a griddle over moderate heat until a drop of water sizzles on the surface. Grease it lightly and, using a ½-cup measure, pour on the batter and smooth quickly with a spatula to a round about 8 to 9 inches in diameter. Brown the crêpe on both sides and remove to a cookie sheet to keep warm in a 200° F. oven until all are made. Sprinkle each crêpe with sugar and fold in four immediately on removing from the griddle.

Chocolate Chocolate Hot Cakes

T*he word chocoholic may not yet be in your dictionary, but it is self-explanatory. Any collection of desserts must have something for the chocoholic, and here is my more-than-just-another-chocolate answer. ~ This is a rich dessert treat for four to six people.*

2 cups cake flour
2 teaspoons baking powder
2 tablespoons sugar
3 tablespoons cocoa
3 large eggs
1¼ cups milk
¼ cup butter, melted
   Confectioners' sugar
   Cinnamon

FILLING
6 (1-ounce) squares semisweet chocolate or 6 ounces semisweet chocolate chips
¾ cup butter
1½ cups confectioners' sugar
6 egg yolks
1½ teaspoons vanilla

Sift the dry ingredients together into a large bowl. In another bowl, beat the eggs and milk together. Whisk them into the dry mixture. When smooth, cover and let rest 1 hour.

Heat a griddle over moderate heat until a drop of water skates over the surface. Fold the melted butter into the batter and drop by tablespoonfuls, stirring before each use. Cook the cakes until they are golden and glazed. Place them on a cookie sheet, stacking or overlapping, until all are made. Cover the cakes with a tea cloth and set them aside.

To make the filling, melt the chocolate and butter together in the top of a double boiler over hot but not boiling water. Remove from the hot water when melted.

In a large bowl, beat the sugar and egg yolks until light and fluffy. Stir in the chocolate mixture and the vanilla. Mix gently and cover the bowl with a cloth and refrigerate 4 hours or more. (This step can be done well in advance of serving.)

To serve, spread half the cakes with the chocolate filling and cover each with a second cake. Serve 3 small sandwiched pancake pairs to each guest. Sift confectioners' sugar over the cakes and sprinkle them lightly with cinnamon.

Chocolate Crêpes with Coconut Cream

*O*ne more chocolate indiscretion—but scheduled at the end of a simple dinner it can't do much harm. And it can be prepared completely in advance, needing only a last-minute twirl of whipped cream. ⁓ This recipe serves four.

¼ cup unsalted butter, melted
2 tablespoons sugar
3 tablespoons cocoa
3 large eggs
1¼ cup milk
1 cup cake flour, sifted
1 cup heavy cream
   Chocolate Curls

FILLING
4 tablespoons cornstarch
⅔ cup sugar
1½ cups milk
2 egg yolks
2 teaspoons vanilla
1 cup flaked coconut

In a large bowl, mix the butter, sugar, and cocoa into a paste. Beat in the eggs, one at a time. Whisk in the milk and flour, alternately. When smooth, cover the batter with a cloth and set it aside for 1 hour in a cool place.

Heat a crêpe pan over moderate heat until a drop of water rolls over the surface. Brush the pan with oil and lift it off the heat. With your other hand, pour in the batter, using a half-filled ¼-cup measure. Swirl the pan and pour any excess batter back into the bowl. Brown the crêpe on both sides and make stacks of 3 or 4 on a cookie sheet. Keep them warm by covering with a cloth until all are finished. There should be 12 crêpes. Set them aside.

To make the filling, blend the cornstarch, sugar, and 1 cup of the milk in a small saucepan. Cook over moderate heat, stirring constantly, until it comes to a boil. Meanwhile, in a small bowl, beat the yolks with the remaining ½ cup milk. Pour in about 2 tablespoonfuls of hot liquid and mix. Gradually beat this into the saucepan mixture, and cook for another minute or until thick. Remove from the heat and stir in the vanilla and coconut. Set it aside to cool.

To assemble, spread each crêpe with a heaping tablespoon of filling, and roll. Arrange on a cookie sheet until all are filled.

In a chilled bowl, beat the heavy cream until stiff. Place 3 crêpes on each dessert plate. Garnish with whipped cream (piped from a pastry bag is nice) and Chocolate Curls.

CHOCOLATE CURLS

Melt 6 ounces of semisweet chocolate squares or chips over hot water. Moving the saucepan to make a band about 18 inches long, pour the melted chocolate onto a baking sheet or marble surface. Spread the chocolate quickly into a strip about 3 inches wide and less than ⅛ inch thick with a flexible metal spatula. Smooth it with the spatula until it begins to set. Let it rest several minutes.

Wedge the baking sheet so that it will not move when you lean your weight behind the blade of a straight-edged knife or metal dough scraper. Starting 1 inch from the near end, hold the blade diagonally to the surface of the chocolate and push the blade away from you. The chocolate should curl up as the blade advances.

Store the curls in layers, separated by waxed paper, in a container in the refrigerator. Broken scraps can be remelted.

Wedding Pancakes with Pistachios

T*hese special pancakes are eaten in the Middle East and Morocco, where they are a feature at weddings and feasts, although with different names and preparation. Called* ataïf *in Egypt and* beghir *in Morocco, they are leavened with yeast and have a spongy texture which soaks up the syrup they are dipped in. They are then spread with clotted cream and sprinkled with chopped pistachio nuts or almonds. For Western appetites, I suggest only the syrup be used or, alternately, apricot preserves thinned with water or Cognac.* ~ *Both are made with semolina, for which the commercial pasta flour sold almost everywhere today is a reasonable substitute; it also adds vitamins and fiber, which compensates a little for the sweetness of the syrup.* ~ *The recipe makes about forty pancakes, enough for a small party eating three or four apiece.*

       1   package dried yeast
       1   teaspoon sugar
    2¼   cups lukewarm water
       2   cups unbleached flour or semolina (pasta flour)
       1   cup apricot preserves
      ½   cup Cognac
       1   cup finely chopped pistachio nuts or almonds

    SYRUP
      ½   cups sugar
    1¼   cups water
    1–2   tablespoons orange-blossom water (see note)

In a large bowl, dissolve the yeast and sugar in ¼ cup of lukewarm water. When it begins to foam, about 10 minutes, add the flour, rubbing it in with the fingers. Add the rest of the water gradually, stirring constantly until the batter is smooth. Cover it with a cloth and leave it to rise in a warm place, about 1 hour.

Meanwhile, make the syrup by combining the sugar, water, and orange-blossom water in a saucepan. Stir over low heat until the sugar is dissolved. Bring to a simmer and cook until it is thick enough to coat the back of a spoon (the soft-ball stage or 234°–240° F. on a candy thermometer). Remove from the heat and let it cool, then refrigerate.

Heat a crêpe pan until a drop of water sizzles on contact with the surface. Lift the pan from the heat and brush it with oil. Pour in 1 tablespoon of batter. Do not spread the batter since the pancake should be a fat little round, not a thin crêpe. When it begins to bubble, flip the cake; when the other side is cooked, set it aside. You may overlap the cakes as they are done.

Put the preserves in a small saucepan. Blend in the Cognac and heat over medium heat, stirring. Cook just long enough to mix thoroughly.

When ready to serve, dip each pancake in the syrup and place 3 or 4 on each serving plate. Dip a small palette knife in the preserves and spread thinly over the 3 or 4 cakes. Sprinkle with nuts and serve.

NOTE: Orange-blossom water is available in Indian specialty stores as well as in pharmacies.

Siamese Coconut Pancakes
~ *Knanom Klok* ~

I n the late eighteenth century, the nation of the T'ai, Siam, was a flourishing kingdom with an elegant and individual cuisine. Although the Siamese ate small amounts at a time, they had frequent meals during the working day. Street vendors sold food all the day long, and among the offerings were thin slices of fruits and fish and chicken and noodles and pancakes. ~ These pancakes are delicious served as a snack, for tea, or with cocoa late at night. Without the sugar, rolled around a teaspoon of peanut butter, they make an interesting accompaniment for drinks. ~ This recipe makes twenty to twenty-four crêpelike pancakes, for four to six people.

> 2   (12-ounce) packages unsweetened coconut flakes
> 1½   cups milk
> ½   cup unbleached, all-purpose flour
> 4   tablespoons sugar
> 4   large eggs, beaten
>   Salt to taste (optional)
>   Confectioners' sugar

Bring the coconut and milk to a boil in a heavy saucepan. Remove from the heat and let it stand for 30 minutes. Strain the liquid into a bowl, pressing the coconut with a spoon, and discard the pulp. Combine the flour and sugar in a bowl and whisk in the strained liquid. Add the beaten eggs, mixing thoroughly, and the salt if desired.

Heat a griddle until a drop of water skates over the surface. Grease it lightly with oil and drop the batter on by tablespoonfuls. Brown each crêpe on both sides and sprinkle with confectioners' sugar while hot. Fold it in three, bringing the sides over the middle.

Peanut Butter Pancakes

T*hese are very popular at children's parties and a good substitute for oversweet cookies and cakes. I would also make them as an after-school snack, and add to the nutritional value by replacing ½ cup of the regular flour with whole-wheat flour. ～ Serve with butter and grape jelly to four to six children, or three to four adults.*

  1 cup chunky peanut butter
  ½ cup butter, melted
  2 large eggs
  1½ cups unbleached, all-purpose flour
  1 teaspoon sugar
  1½ teaspoons baking powder
    Pinch of salt (optional)
  1½ cups milk

In a large bowl, beat together the peanut butter and butter until smooth. Beat in the eggs, one at a time. In another bowl, sift the dry ingredients together. Add the flour mixture to the egg mixture alternately with the milk. Stir until thoroughly combined and let the batter rest 1 hour covered with a cloth.

Heat a griddle until a drop of water skates over the surface. Grease it lightly and, using a full ¼-cup measure, drop the batter onto the griddle to form rounds approximately 3 inches in diameter.

Keep the cakes hot on a cookie sheet or in an ovenproof dish in a 200° F. oven until all are made.

A Fat Broiled Pancake with Pecans

O*n my first trip to San Francisco in 1983, I had a list of places absolutely not to miss—no trolley cars, no Golden Gate Bridge —all of them to do with food. The most important thing to me was to track down Jack Lirio, whose book* Cooking with Jack Lirio *had come out the year before. With his training in China and France, his recipes were innovative, classically based, and beautifully presented. This one is an example. ⁓ These pancakes can be started several hours before dinner; the final fifteen-minute assembly makes it possible to serve them warm to the eagerly waiting, or watching, guests. Each of the two pancakes this recipe makes divides into four wedges. They can also be served cold, spread with butter and sprinkled with confectioners' sugar. ⁓ This recipe serves eight.*

　¾　cup unbleached, all-purpose flour
　¾　cup whole-wheat flour
　　　Salt to taste
　¾　cup nonfat milk
　¼　cup heavy cream
　3　tablespoons butter
　2　cups pecans, whole or in pieces
　4　large eggs, separated
　1　tablespoon sugar

HOT MAPLE SYRUP
　1　cup dark brown or white sugar
　½　cup water
　2　tablespoons butter
　¼　tablespoon maple flavoring

Sift the flours and salt into a large bowl.

In a small heavy saucepan, mix the milk, cream, and butter. Over low heat, bring the milk mixture to 98° F. on a thermometer or just warm enough to feel warm to a fingertip. The butter will melt as the mixture sits, covered, until the final assembly.

On a plate or pan, divide the pecans into 4 portions, about ½ cup in each mound. (The preparation can be interrupted at this point, with the eggs out of the refrigerator to come to room temperature.)

Whisk the milk mixture into the flours, and beat until smooth. In another bowl, beat egg yolks until light and thick. Fold into the batter.

Preheat the broiler.

Whip egg whites until stiff but not dry, and fold into the batter.

Heat a 9-inch skillet over medium heat until hot enough to make a drop of water sizzle on contact. Brush with oil and sprinkle one portion of the pecans over the bottom. Pour in half of the batter, being careful not to disturb the pecans. Smooth the top and sprinkle over another portion of pecans.

Slide the skillet under the broiler, 7 to 8 inches from the heat. Cook until the cake is brown, about 4 minutes. Loosen the edges with a spatula and turn the pancake over with the spatula. (This will not be difficult because the cake will be very firm.) Sprinkle ½ tablespoon of sugar over the top and return the pan to the broiler to brown the top. It will take only about 1 minute.

Turn the pancake onto a plate and cover with a towel until the second pancake is made by the same procedure.

While the pancakes cook, prepare the sauce: mix the sugar and water in a small heavy saucepan. Bring them to a boil over moderate heat and continue boiling for 5 minutes. Remove from the heat and when the syrup is still quite warm, add the butter and stir until mixed in. Beat in the flavoring. Cut each pancake in 4 wedges, top with syrup and serve immediately.

Swedish Pancakes with Crushed Strawberries

During the years I had my model agency in Paris, I frequently visited Sweden and Denmark, hunting the fabled, long-legged Scandinavian beauty—and found her, too, but that's another story. While in Stockholm I dined at the Operkällaren and other elegant dining places, and was also fortunate enough to be invited to eat in private homes. Whenever I was asked what I would like as dessert, I begged for plättar—Swedish pancakes. ⁓ These are traditionally eaten with the Nordic fruit lingonberries, which look like red currants and taste like cranberries, but I prefer crushed strawberries when I can find them really ripe, with a dash of Kirsch, or white crème de menthe. ⁓ The Swedish pancake pan, plättpan, is absolutely essential for making these. It can be found in kitchen specialty stores nationwide, and can be used with other pancake batter as well. For parties, it is a splendid way to make perfectly shaped blini. After all, Russia and Sweden are not too far apart on the globe. ⁓ This recipe makes about thirty small cakes, enough for four servings.

> 1 quart ripe strawberries
> 3 tablespoons Kirsch or white crème de menthe *or* ¼ cup confectioners' sugar

> PANCAKES
> 3 tablespoons butter
> ½ cup water
> ½ cup unbleached, all-purpose flour
> 3 large eggs
> 1 cup milk
> 1 teaspoon vanilla
> Melted butter for cooking

Wash and hull the strawberries. Slice them thinly into a glass serving bowl. Crush them slightly with a potato masher or fork, and sprinkle the liqueur or sugar over them. Mix thoroughly and let macerate at room temperature for 1 hour.

To make the pancakes, combine the butter and water in a small saucepan. Bring them to a boil and remove from the heat. Add the flour all at once and stir vigorously until it is completely absorbed. Return the pan to a low heat and, stirring constantly, cook for 2 minutes or until the paste pulls away from the sides of the pan. Remove from the heat and transfer to a medium-sized bowl.

Beat in the eggs, one at a time, being sure each is absorbed before adding the next. Beat in the milk, mixing thoroughly. Beat in the vanilla and set the batter aside while preparing the pan.

Heat a *plättpan* until very hot but not smoking. Brush each indentation with butter and lift off the heat. Drop a mounded tablespoon of batter into each indentation, spreading it with the back of the spoon. Return the pan to the heat and brown the cakes on the bottom. Turn them with a small spatula and brown them on the other side. Line the cakes up on a cookie sheet; do not stack them. Keep them warm in a 200° F. oven until all are made. Serve 6 or 7 to each person, passing the strawberry sauce separately.

The Emperor's Folly

~ *Kaiserschmarren* ~

N o one seems to know why this delightful pancake is called The Emperor's Folly. The method of making it is unique in the world of cuisine and it appears in all the old German cookbooks. I received this particular recipe from a young German colleague who had it from her family archives. ~ The folly seems to be tearing the pancake apart with forks when it is only lightly set, but magically, with butter and sugar, the pieces hold together in a scrambled fashion. To serve, the confection is separated into wedges with two forks. ~ It will be enough for four people.

½   cup raisins

3   tablespoons rum

1½ cup unbleached, all-purpose flour
     Pinch of salt

4   large eggs, separated

2   tablespoons sugar

1⅔ cups milk

6   tablespoons butter, 2 melted

2   tablespoons grated lemon peel

¼   cup confectioners' sugar

In a small bowl, soak the raisins in the rum for 30 minutes.

Sift the flour and salt into a large bowl. Beat the egg yolks with the sugar in a medium bowl until light in color. Add the milk, the 2 tablespoons of melted butter, and the lemon peel to the yolk mixture. Whisk this mixture into the flour. Fold in the raisins and the rum.

Whip the egg whites until stiff but not dry. Fold them gently into the batter.

Melt 1 tablespoon of the remaining butter in a heavy skillet over medium heat and pour in half the batter. When the bottom of the pancake is barely cooked but not brown, about 3 minutes, tear it with two forks into pieces no bigger than a silver dollar. Sprinkle generously with powdered sugar and cook until the bottom is golden. Slide the cake onto a plate and add 1 tablespoon of butter to the pan. When it is melted, reverse the pancake into the pan using two large spatulas. Sprinkle again with powdered sugar and continue to cook it until the underside is golden, about 1 or 2 minutes. Turn the cake out on a heatproof platter and keep it warm in a 200° F. oven. Make the other half of the batter into a pancake in the same fashion.

To serve, separate the cakes into wedges with two forks and sprinkle with confectioners' sugar.

VARIATION: For *Apfelschmarren,* or Apple Folly, substitute for the raisins 4 ripe apples sautéed in ¼ cup butter.

The Big Apple Pancake
~ La Crêpiaud Normande ~

When you consider that any breakfast pancake can become an apple pancake just by adding thin apple slices to the batter, it increases the wonder that apple pancakes can be glamorous desserts, widely different from one another. Just as the pancake itself can change from homely breakfast fare to fabulous crêpe creations, so the humble apple, available everywhere at every season, can make the same metamorphosis. ~ In France the adjective Normande *on any menu reveals the presence of apples because Normandy is the apple capital of the country, just as New York is the Big Apple in the United States.* La Crêpiaud Normande *therefore means "The Big Apple Pancake" and it is a traditional feature of the Cuisine Bonne Femme, French home cooking.* ~ This recipe is from my favorite small Parisian restaurant, La Cafétière. In Normandy the pancake is cooked in an iron skillet over an open fire and is accompanied by glasses of Calvados, the local apple brandy. ~ This serves four to six people.

    1 cup sugar
    ⅓ cup water
    5 Golden Delicious apples
    4 large eggs
    1 cup heavy cream
    ¼ teaspoon mace
    ¼ teaspoon allspice
    1 cup unbleached, all-purpose flour
    2 tablespoons Calvados or applejack

In a small heavy saucepan, swirl the sugar and water over medium heat until the sugar is dissolved. Cook, covered, for 1 minute. Remove the cover and let the syrup boil until the soft-ball stage is reached, 234° to 240° F. on a candy thermometer. Pour at once into a 10-inch ovenproof skillet or 10-inch glass pie pan.

Preheat the oven to 400° F.

Pare and core the apples and cut each into 12 sections. Arrange them on the syrup and place the skillet over medium heat. (If using a glass pan, you will need a heat protector underneath it.) Slowly bring the syrup to a bubble. Meanwhile, whisk together the batter ingredients.

When the syrup is golden brown, remove it from the heat. Pour the batter over the apples and return to the heat. When the batter is set, 4 to 5 minutes, slide the pan or skillet into the oven.

When the pancake top is brown and crusty, 5 to 10 minutes, remove the pan from the oven and, holding a serving plate against the pan, reverse the two, turning the pancake upside down onto the plate. Cut the pancake into 4 to 6 wedges and serve immediately.

Cranberry Souffléed Pancakes

his is a very pretty end to a dinner and one that can be prepared up to the last 10 minutes, plenty of time for the hostess-chef to slip into the kitchen while the guests eat their salads. The orange marmalade sauce can be made ahead of time and briefly reheated while the second pancake is broiling. Even better would be to have two skillets. ~ Instead of cranberries, poached pear slices or dried fruit, caramelized apples (page 37), or fresh plums or peaches might be used. With these fruits, the step with the boiling syrup can be omitted and apricot preserves substituted for the marmalade in the dessert sauce. ~ This recipe serves eight.

3 large eggs, separated

2 tablespoons Grand Marnier or other orange-flavored liqueur

½ cup unbleached, all-purpose flour

Salt to taste (optional)

½ cup heavy cream

2 tablespoons milk

1 cup sugar

½ cup water

1 (12 ounce) package cranberries

2 tablespoons clarified butter (see Note)

Butter for brushing

DESSERT SAUCE

½ cup orange marmalade or apricot preserves

2 tablespoons orange-flavored or other fruit liqueur

In a large bowl, beat the egg yolks with the liqueur until thick and lemon colored. Whisk in the flour, salt if desired, then the cream and milk. Mix only until just combined; set aside.

In a heavy saucepan, bring the sugar and water to a boil. Reduce the heat and simmer, stirring, until the sugar is dissolved. Increase the heat to medium and add the cranberries all at once. Cook until most of the berries have burst, about 5 minutes. Remove from the heat and cool. (If you wish, you may now make the dessert sauce and refrigerate all three elements until ready to whip the egg whites and fold into the batter.)

To make the sauce, put the marmalade and liqueur into a small heavy saucepan. Cook them over medium heat, stirring, until completely mixed, about 3 minutes. Remove from the heat and cool. If you wish, you may now refrigerate the batter, berries, and sauce until just before baking.

When ready to serve the pancakes, preheat the broiler.

Whip the egg whites until stiff but not dry, and fold them into the batter. Fold in the clarified butter.

Heat a 9-inch skillet over medium heat until a drop of water skates over the surface. Brush generously with butter and pour in half the batter, spreading it evenly. Cook for 3 minutes and remove from the heat. Spread half the cranberries over the surface and slide the skillet under the broiler, 5 inches from the heat, for 1 to 2 minutes or until puffed and brown. Slip the pancake onto a serving dish and keep it on top of the stove to stay warm. Make the second pancake and reheat the sauce.

Cut each pancake in 4 wedges and place 1 teaspoon of sauce alongside each serving. Pass the rest of the sauce.

NOTE: To make clarified butter, melt unsalted butter over very low heat in a small heavy saucepan, watching that it does not brown. Remove from the heat and let it stand a few minutes until the milky solids settle to the bottom. Skim off the clear butter into a glass jar and store, covered, for weeks. One half cup of butter will make about ⅓ cup of clarified butter.

Kiwi Blini with Pomegranate Syrup

I could have christened this recipe Blini with Chinese Gooseberries, which is the kiwi's name in its homeland, China. It comes to our markets from New Zealand, where it was renamed, probably by a Maori farmer, after the strange flightless kiwi bird. ～ At first the kiwi fruit was a rare and exotic sight in our fruit markets, but modern distribution efficiency has made it a very affordable novelty. It has a sweet-sour taste which makes it just right for these dessert blini. ～ The recipe makes thirty or more 2½-inch rounds, enough for six lovely desserts with the pretty contrast of the Grenadine or pomegranate syrup.

½ package dried yeast
4 tablespoons lukewarm water
1 tablespoon sugar
  Pinch of salt (optional)
2 large eggs, lightly beaten
1½ cups unbleached, all-purpose flour
1 cup milk
3 tablespoons butter, melted, or vegetable oil
3 or 4 kiwis, *firm*, not soft
  Pomegranate Syrup
  Yogurt Cheese (page 39), optional

Sprinkle the yeast over the water in a large bowl. Stir in the sugar and let sit for 10 minutes. Whisk in the eggs, then the flour and milk alternately in 2 or 3 batches. Add the butter and beat until the batter is smooth. Cover with a cloth and set aside to rise in a warm, draft-free place, about 45 minutes.

When the batter is ready, peel the fruit thinly and slice it ⅛ inch thick. Arrange the slices on paper towels.

Heat a griddle over low heat until a drop of water sizzles on contact and brush lightly with oil. Stir down the batter and, using a measuring tablespoon, drop the batter on the griddle. While the first side is cooking, take a slice of kiwi in your fingers, draw it across the batter, and place it, bare side down, on the blini. When bubbles appear, turn the cakes with a spatula or pancake turner and cook the other side, a matter of 10 seconds or so. Arrange on a towel-lined baking sheet and keep them in a barely warm oven (125°–150° F.).

Pour enough syrup on each dessert plate to barely cover it, arrange 5 or 6 blini on it, fruit side up, and spread with Yogurt Cheese if desired. Pass the rest of the syrup in a small pitcher.

POMEGRANATE SYRUP
~

 ¾ cup sugar
1½ cups water
 3 tablespoons Grenadine syrup

Bring the sugar and water to a boil, stirring until the sugar is dissolved. Continue to boil for 3 to 5 minutes and remove from heat. When it is cool, stir in the Grenadine. Serve at room temperature. ~ This will make about 1¼ cups.

Corinthian Crêpes

T hese delicious crêpes, despite their Greek name, are a French specialty. In our Colonial days, currants were called "raisins from Corinth," just as they are today in France. This was because the tiny, dried fruit came from the port of Corinth to the rest of the world, but nowadays California rivals the Middle East's production of them. ⁓ The recipe makes fifteen to eighteen crêpes, for five to six servings.

> 2 cups milk
> 1¾ cups unbleached, all-purpose flour
> 3 large eggs, well beaten
> 4 tablespoons butter, melted
> Zest of 1 orange, julienned
> ¼ cup dark rum
> ½ cup dried currants
> Butter for cooking

> APRICOT SAUCE
> 1 cup apricot preserves
> 2 tablespoons sugar
> 2 tablespoons dark rum

In a large bowl, whisk the milk into the flour until combined. Beat in the eggs, 2 tablespoonfuls at a time. Add the butter and beat until smooth, straining through a sieve if lumpy.

In a small saucepan, simmer the slivers of orange peel in the rum for 5 minutes. Remove the peel with a slotted spoon and reserve the rum. Put the currants into the warm rum and let them macerate at least 1 hour.

Meanwhile, make the sauce. Heat the sauce ingredients in a small heavy saucepan until they begin to bubble. Remove from the heat and pass through a coarse sieve, rubbing with the back of a spoon to force the fruit through. Set the sauce aside and keep it warm over hot water.

Stir the plumped currants into the crêpe batter. Heat a crêpe pan until a drop of water dances on the surface. Lift the pan off the heat and brush it with butter. With the other hand, using a half-filled ¼-cup measure, pour the batter into the pan and swirl to spread the batter evenly. Pour any excess back into the bowl. Cook until the crêpe is golden on both sides. Fold the finished crêpes in quarters and keep them warm in an ovenproof dish in a 200° F. oven.

Serve 2 or 3 to each person with apricot sauce spooned over the tops.

Cha Cha Cha
Banana Pancakes

I was in Jamaica only once but I shall always remember that island. I loved the food, the people, the scenery. I couldn't believe that the philodendron, that costly plant in the luxury apartments of New York, grew unconcernedly along the roadsides. ~ After dancing all night at an Ocho Rios nightclub one star-spangled evening, I left with the beautiful owner to have breakfast. He was six foot six, an Oxford graduate, a great dancer, and, I learned, a great cook. ~ When I returned at dawn, the posh hotel in Montego Bay invited me to leave the next day for "fraternizing with the natives." Of course, this happened in the fifties before the government changed. And about time, too! ~ This recipe serves two people, but can be doubled or tripled.

1 ripe banana, mashed
1 tablespoon sugar
1 large egg, beaten
3 tablespoons unbleached, all-purpose flour
3 tablespoons butter
   Juice of 1 lime
   Powdered sugar

Whisk the banana, sugar, and egg together. Sift the flour over the mixture and fold together.

Heat a skillet or griddle over moderate heat until a drop of water sizzles on contact. Melt 1 tablespoon of butter in the skillet and drop the batter on by tablespoonfuls. Brown the pancakes on both sides and serve immediately, sprinkled with the juice and sugar. Butter the skillet as needed.

Papaya
Cream-Filled Crêpes

P*apayas have been called tree melons, and they do have a similar, refreshing taste. They can be bought almost entirely green and left to ripen in the kitchen to a beautiful apricot color. Once all golden, they must be refrigerated until needed. ～ This luscious and sinfully easy recipe can also be poured into tulip cups (page 54) made with dessert crêpes and baked for 20 minutes, then served with more diced papaya on top. ～ The recipe makes 2 to 2¼ cups of the cream, and serves four.*

     1 ripe papaya
       Juice of 1 lime
     1 (14 ounce) can sweetened condensed milk
     8 Basic Dessert Crêpes (page 82)
     1 navel orange

Slice the papaya in half and remove the seeds and any fibers with a spoon. Peel and dice the flesh. Place it in a small bowl and mix thoroughly with the lime juice. Cover with plastic wrap and let macerate at room temperature 1 hour.

Place the fruit and juice in a food processor or food mill. Pour the contents of the can of condensed milk into the processor, and purée 1 or 2 minutes. If using a food mill, pass the fruit through with the lime juice into a bowl, and beat in the condensed milk.

Spread the papaya cream over half of each crêpe and fold over. Arrange 2 crêpes back to back on each of 4 dessert plates. Peel the orange, removing all the white pith. Cut four ⅛-inch slices and place one on each plate. Spoon a little papaya cream across the crêpes and serve.

Praline Soufflé Crêpes

A dessert soufflé, despite the awe and mystery surrounding it, is nothing more than a pastry cream with the egg whites beaten stiff and folded into the yolk mixture. Since this simple recipe can be made in two stages, the last taking only 4 or 5 minutes before baking the crêpes, you will be a magician as well as a master chef in your guests' eyes on presenting this glamorous result. The only garnish they need besides your lovely dessert plates is perhaps a single slice of star fruit, or a flower. The praline flavoring in this recipe may be replaced by vanilla or almond extract. ~ This amount will fill eight crêpes, or two each for four people.

4 tablespoons unsalted butter
3 tablespoons unbleached, all-purpose flour
1 teaspoon cornstarch
1 cup hot milk
3 large egg yolks
4 large egg whites
½ cup sugar
4 tablespoons Praline Powder
8 Basic Dessert Crêpes (page 82)

In a heavy saucepan, melt the butter over low heat. Stir in the flour and cornstarch and cook for 3 minutes, stirring constantly. Whisk in the mik and continue stirring for 5 minutes. Beat the yolks in a small bowl. Stir in 2 tablespoons of the hot liquid and then pour the mixture into the saucepan. Stir over low heat until very thick, about 8 to 10 minutes. Remove from heat and cover the surface with plastic wrap. The batter may stand 30 minutes at room temperature.

Preheat the oven to 350° F. In a large bowl, whisk the egg whites until soft peaks form. Continue whisking while adding the sugar in a steady stream until stiff peaks are formed. Fold one third thoroughly into the yolk mixture, then pour this into the rest of the whites. Fold together gently; fold in the Praline Powder.

Spread about 2 tablespoons of the soufflé mixture on half of each crêpe, ½-inch thick. Fold the other half over lightly, making sure it adheres to the soufflé filling. Arrange on a baking sheet. Bake for 10 to 12 minutes or until puffed and golden. (Meanwhile, you may join your guests for the salad course even though keeping an eye on your watch.) Serve the crêpes immediately.

PRALINE POWDER
~

1 cup sugar

3 tablespoons water

½ cup blanched almonds or hazelnuts

In a small heavy saucepan, dissolve the sugar in the water by stirring over medium heat. Cook until it is a golden caramel color. Stir in the nuts and turn out onto a lightly oiled baking sheet to cool and harden. When hard, break in pieces and pulverize in a food processor or blender until finely powdered. The powder will keep in an airtight jar indefinitely. ~ This makes about 1 cup.

Double Berry Crêpes

Here is another dessert that can be put together in minutes with defrosted dessert crêpes from the freezer. Any berry that's in season can be used. The amount of sugar needed will vary according to the ripeness and sweetness of the berries. Tasting is the only way to judge. ~ Serve this to four people.

1 quart raspberries, strawberries, or blueberries, or puréed fruit

4 tablespoons Kirsch or other fruit liqueur

½ cup confectioners' sugar or to taste

8 Basic Dessert Crêpes (page 82)

1 cup heavy cream, whipped (optional), or *crème fraîche* (page 63)

Slice the berries into a large bowl and crush slightly with a potato masher or fork. Stir in the liqueur and sugar and let macerate for 1 hour at room temperature.

When ready to serve, drain the fruit, reserving the juice. Purée one half of the fruit in a food processor or food mill, adding the reserved juice.

Divide the remaining crushed fruit between the 8 crêpes and roll. Place 2 crêpes, seam side down, on each of 4 plates. Spoon the puréed berries over them and serve with whipped cream, if desired.

VARIATIONS: Puréed fruit. Almost any fruit, from familiar native fruits like apricots, peaches, pears, and nectarines to exotic mangoes and papayas, make delightful fillings for dessert or breakfast crêpes. Most fruits must be poached in a simple syrup before puréeing, but many need only the addition of orange juice and even a dash of fruit liqueur. Berries, as in the recipe above, are the easiest of all, simply crushed with sugar or lemon juice added to taste. All should be served at room temperature.

MANGOES AND PAPAYAS

~

2 ripe mangoes or papayas

1 cup fresh orange juice

1 tablespoon orange liqueur
  (optional)

Buy soft mangoes or let them soften in the kitchen like an avocado. The same is true of the papaya, except that it must have some evidence of its final golden color, even if only a streak of yellow. It will turn to gold after a few days. Halve the fruit (this may be messy) and remove the seeds. Scrape the flesh into the container of a food processor, blender, or food mill. Add the orange juice while the machine is going and purée until smooth. If using a food mill, pass the pulp through and fold in the juice, beating until smooth. Stir in the liqueur, if desired. ~ This should make 2 cups of purée.

RHUBARB

~

1 pound rhubarb

½ cup sugar

Juice of 1 lemon

Wash the rhubarb and cut into 2-inch lengths. In a medium-size bowl, mix the rhubarb pieces with the sugar and lemon juice. Let it stand until sugar is dissolved, about 15 minutes. Place the mixture in a heavy saucepan and bring to a simmer over moderate heat. Cook slowly until the fruit is soft, about 30 minutes, stirring occasionally. Remove from the heat and let cool. Purée in a food processor or pass through a food mill. ~ This makes from 1½ to 2 cups of purée.

A delicious variation is to add 1 pint of strawberries after 20 minutes of simmering, and process all together. This may be served warm or cold.

APRICOTS, NECTARINES, PEACHES, APPLES, PEARS, PLUMS

~

1 pound fruit all together

½ cup water

1 cup sugar

Peel the fruit (except for plums) thinly and core or remove the pits. (Apples, nectarines, and peaches can be peeled more easily when they've been dropped into boiling water for 1 minute, then plunged into cold water.)

In a small heavy saucepan, mix the sugar and water and stir over moderate heat until the sugar is dissolved, about 3 minutes. Bring to a boil and cook for 2 minutes; remove from the heat. Let cool before adding the fruit.

Slice the fruit into the saucepan containing the syrup and bring to a simmer over low heat. Cook until heated through, about 5 minutes for plums and apricots, 10 minutes for peaches and nectarines, or until soft. Pass the fruit through a food mill or whirl in a food processor. Cinnamon, cloves, nutmeg, freshly ground pepper, or vanilla may be stirred in. ~ This will make about 2 cups of purée.

VARIATION: Sugarless Applesauce. For a healthy pancake topping or filling, prepare as above, eliminating the sugar, halving the water, and leaving the skins on the apples. For more texture, mash the fruit with a fork instead of puréeing.

Cherry Meringue Crêpes

T *o be really theatrical, you may flambé these crêpes, but even without the flames of brandy and Kirsch, they are beautifully dramatic. An equal amount of any canned or cooked fruit may be substituted for the sour cherries.* ⁓ *There are two crêpes for each of four people.*

        2 cups pitted sour cherries
       ½ cup sugar
           Dash of cinnamon
        1 tablespoon cornstarch
        3 large egg whites
        5 tablespoons sugar
       ⅓ cup ground hazelnuts
        8 Basic Dessert Crêpes (page 82)
        3 tablespoons Kirsch (optional)
        3 tablespoons brandy (optional)

Combine the cherries, sugar, cinnamon, and ½ cup of water in a heavy saucepan and bring to a boil. Reduce the heat to a simmer and let stew, covered, for 5 minutes. Mix the cornstarch with 1 tablespoon of water and stir into the cherries. Let it cook over low heat until thickened. Remove the cherries with a slotted spoon, reserving the juice, and divide between the crêpes; roll each crêpe up. Spread the reserved juice in an ovenproof dish and fit in the rolls. Preheat the oven to 425° F.

Whip the egg whites until soft peaks form. Sprinkle in the sugar and ground nuts slowly, continuing to beat until the meringue is stiff. Pile the meringue on the crêpes, pulling it into decorative peaks with a fork. Bake until the meringue is golden. Serve immediately, 2 per person. If you wish to add extra pizzazz, heat the Kirsch and brandy together. Pour over the dish and light.

Souffléed Crêpes with
Walnuts and Chocolate Sauce

During the sixteen years I had my model agency in Paris, I traveled about Europe searching for beautiful faces and made it a rule to be in Munich a few weeks before Christmas. Just to enter the doors of Dahlmeyer's famous delicatessen is to step into the magic land of Santa Claus. Joseph Hergesheimer, the noted gastronome, once said that if the people in Munich are not eating, they are thinking about it. These crêpes are symbolic of that preoccupation. ∼ The filling is enough for eight sandwichlike servings.

WALNUT FILLING
½ cup strawberry preserves
½ cup walnuts, coarsely chopped
2 tablespoons heavy cream
2 tablespoons Grand Marnier or other orange liqueur

CHOCOLATE SAUCE
6 ounces (6 squares) semisweet chocolate
4 tablespoons (½ stick) butter
1 tablespoon Grand Marnier or other orange-flavored liqueur
4 tablespoons butter
1 cup milk
½ cup unbleached, all-purpose flour
5 large eggs, separated
   Zest of 1 lemon, grated
1 teaspoon vanilla
1 tablespoon Cognac
3 tablespoons sugar
   Raspberries or strawberries for garnish (optional)

To make the walnut filling, combine all the ingredients thoroughly in a small heavy saucepan. Cook them over medium heat until just heated through. Cool and set aside.

To make the chocolate sauce, melt all the ingredients together over hot water and keep hot.

Combine the butter and milk in a heavy saucepan and bring slowly to scalding. Let simmer until the butter is melted and remove from the heat. Add the flour all at once and stir with a wooden spoon. When combined, return to the heat and stir until the mixture pulls away from the sides of the pan.

Remove from the heat again and beat in the egg yolks, one at a time, beating until each is completely absorbed into the batter. Beat in the lemon, vanilla, and Cognac.

In another bowl, whisk the egg whites until foamy and sprinkle in the sugar. Beat until the meringue holds its shape on the beater. Mix one quarter of the meringue into the batter to lighten, then fold in the rest.

Heat a griddle over medium heat until hot enough to make a drop of water sizzle on contact. Drop the batter by heaping tablespoonfuls and smooth evenly with the back of the spoon. Turn after 1 minute and brown the other side. Stack on a baking sheet until all are made. There should be eight crêpes.

To assemble, spread each crêpe with 2 tablespoons of the filling. Place it on a serving plate, top with another crêpe, and spoon chocolate sauce over each sandwich. Garnish, if desired, with raspberries or a strawberry.

Nutty Crêpes with Crème Chantilly

These crêpes can be made ahead of a fancy dinner party and refrigerated. At the last moment, just before sitting down with your guests for the first course, you can assemble the crêpes and leave them in the refrigerator until time to serve. ~ The recipe makes eighteen to twenty crêpes, and can be served in stacks of two or three, depending on the number of guests.

½ cup walnuts or skinned hazelnuts, ground fine but not to a powder

1 cup unbleached, all-purpose flour

1¼ cups milk

4 large eggs

2 tablespoons honey

Pinch of mace

Pinch of black pepper

Pastry Cream

CRÈME CHANTILLY

1 cup heavy cream

1 tablespoon confectioners' sugar

4 1-ounce squares semisweet chocolate, grated

Combine the ground nuts and the flour in a medium-size bowl. In another bowl, blend the milk, eggs, and honey together and beat until smooth.

Whisk the liquid mixture into the flour and mix thoroughly. Season to taste with mace and pepper and let rest, covered, for 1 hour.

Meanwhile, make the Pastry Cream; cool before refrigerating.

Heat a crêpe pan over medium heat until a drop of water dances on the surface. Brush with butter and lift off the heat. With the other hand, half-fill a ¼-cup measure with batter and pour into the pan, swirling it to spread the batter evenly. Pour any excess back into the bowl. Brown the crêpes on both sides and stack them on a cookie sheet until all are made. (If making them more than 2 days before they are to be served, wrap them together in plastic wrap in batches of 8 and freeze. Defrost them at room temperature.)

To assemble, whip the heavy cream with the confectioners' sugar in a large bowl until stiff peaks form. Make stacks of 2 or 3 crêpes with a scant tablespoon of Pastry Cream spread between each layer. With a pastry bag, decorate the top of each stack with rosettes of whipped cream. Sprinkle with grated chocolate and serve.

PASTRY CREAM

½ cup milk

3 tablespoons sugar

2 large egg yolks

2 teaspoons unbleached, all-
   purpose flour

1 teaspoon cornstarch

½ cup heavy cream, softly whipped

½ teaspoon vanilla

Scald the milk and 2 tablespoons of the sugar in a small heavy saucepan. In a medium-size bowl, beat the egg yolks with the remaining tablespoon of sugar until light colored. Beat in the flour and cornstarch and mix well. Beat in half the hot milk and pour the mixture into the saucepan. Bring to a boil over medium heat, whisking continually. Cook 1 minute and remove from the heat. Pour into a bowl to cool and cover the surface with plastic wrap. Immediately before using, fold in the softly whipped cream and vanilla. ∼ This recipe makes 1¼ cups.

Crêpes Suzy Flambées with Tangerines

C rêpes Suzette are such a classic that sophisticated gourmets consider the dessert a cliché, and yet, like all clichés, they have become that only because of their intrinsic truth or, in this case, goodness. ～ I am dedicating my version of the classic to my sister Suzy, not only because of her marvelous tangerine-colored hair, but because I think the flaming part of the dish will appeal to her dramatic as well as her culinary talents. ～ This will serve four.

> 3 tangerines (firm, not loose in their skins)
> 7 tablespoons sugar
> ½ cup tangerine or orange juice
> 4 tablespoons unsalted butter
> 2 teaspoons cornstarch
> 12 Basic Dessert Crêpes (page 82)
>   Butter for the baking dish
> ¼ cup Cointreau or other orange or tangerine liqueur
> ¼ cup Cognac

Peel the tangerines, reserving the skin of 1 of them. Whirl this skin in a food processor or blender with 4 tablespoons of sugar and 2 tablespoons of the juice until a fine paste is formed.

Melt the butter in a heavy skillet and add the sugar mixture, stirring until the sugar is melted. Dissolve the cornstarch in the rest of the juice. Lower the heat and whisk the liquid into the sugar mixture. Let it simmer until thickened, stirring constantly. Remove from the heat.

Separate the tangerines into sections, carefully removing the white pith. Add the fruit to the skillet and cook over medium heat until warmed through, about 5 minutes. Remove from the heat and set aside to cool.

Preheat the oven to 350° F.

Divide the sauce with the tangerine sections between the 12 crêpes. Fold in quarters and arrange, overlapping slightly, in a buttered baking dish. (You may cover them and refrigerate until ready to serve, at this point, if desired.)

Before serving, sprinkle the crêpes with the remaining 3 tablespoons of sugar and place them in the upper third of the oven. Bake them until the sugar begins to caramelize lightly, about 10 to 15 minutes.

Meanwhile, warm the Cointreau and Cognac in a small saucepan. Remove the crêpes from the oven when ready and pour on the warm liqueurs. Immediately, carry them to the table and ignite the liqueur. While it is flaming, spoon it over the crêpes. Serve 3 to a person when the flames have died down.

Index